T0385496

Design for Change in Higher Education

DESIGN for *CHANGE* in HIGHER EDUCATION

JEFFREY T. GRABILL
SARAH GRETTER
ERIK SKOGSBERG

JOHNS HOPKINS UNIVERSITY PRESS | *Baltimore*

© 2022 Johns Hopkins University Press
All rights reserved. Published 2022
Printed in the United States of America on acid-free paper

2 4 6 8 9 7 5 3 1

Johns Hopkins University Press
2715 North Charles Street
Baltimore, Maryland 21218-4363
www.press.jhu.edu

Library of Congress Cataloging-in-Publication Data

Names: Grabill, Jeffrey T., 1968– author. | Gretter, Sarah, author. |
Skogsberg, Erik, 1983– author.
Title: Design for change in higher education / Jeffrey T. Grabill, Sarah Gretter,
Erik Skogsberg.
Description: Baltimore : Johns Hopkins University Press, 2022. |
Includes bibliographical references and index.
Identifiers: LCCN 2021018591 | ISBN 9781421443218 (hardcover) |
ISBN 9781421443225 (ebook)
Subjects: LCSH: Universities and colleges—United States—Administration. |
Instructional systems—United States—Design. | Educational change—
United States. | Organizational change—United States.
Classification: LCC LB2341 .G667 2022 | DDC 378.1/01—dc23
LC record available at https://lccn.loc.gov/2021018591

A catalog record for this book is available from the British Library.

*Special discounts are available for bulk purchases of this book. For more information,
please contact Special Sales at specialsales@jh.edu.*

Jeff: For Chandra, Megan, and Jackson, always. And to Sarah and Erik, who responded with grace to the statement "we need to write this book . . . now."

Sarah: I simply want to thank my boys, Isaac and Victor, for their patience with me during this process (in the middle of the 2020 pandemic), and I would like to dedicate this book to my dad, Marc Gretter, who passed this year. Finally, I'd like to thank Caroline and Ashley, who have been amazing colleagues (and friends) to brainstorm playbook ideas with over the past years.

Erik: This book is for my Dad, Keith Skogsberg, who passed suddenly this year. He was my first designer. From an early age, I spent time in his woodshop, witnessing continuous problem-framing, prototyping, and iteration. And he always did it with such joy.

CONTENTS

Acknowledgments ix

Introduction. Designing Change in Higher Education   1

1. Learning Experience Design in Higher Education   23

2. Operationalizing Design   42

3. Designing Conversations   64

4. Change Management as Design   84

5. Assessment and Research in a Higher Education
Design Organization   105
WILLIAM F. HEINRICH AND REBECCA L. MATZ

6. Designing Requires a Design Organization   124

Notes   143
Index   159

ACKNOWLEDGMENTS

The contributions to this book extend far beyond the three of us. This book is possible because of the shared work of the Hub team. They should see themselves and their contributions in the narrative, and this community has been a constant source of support, brain power, and collegiality. Thank you, Devon Akmon, Claire Banyas, Ashley Braman, Erin Brown, Emilio Esposito, Dave Goodrich, Brendan Guenther, Darren Hood, Summer Issawi, Alicia Jenner, Talitha Johnson, Michael Lockett, Jay Loftus, Ellie Louson, Angie Martin, Kelly Mazurkiewicz, Natasha Miller, Rashad Muhammad, Makena Neal, Julie Orler, Jerry Rhead, Antajuan Scott, Mark Sullivan, Ryan Sweeder, Greg Teachout, Erica Venton, Caroline White, and Bre Yaklin.

We're also immensely grateful to past Hub colleagues who have contributed to the mission and vision of the Hub and to the work in this playbook: Bill Hart-Davidson, Teal Amthor-Shaffer, James Bender, Alyssa Bradley, Emily Brozovic, Chloe Foster, Molly Frendo, Leigh Graves Wolf, April Greenwood, Susan Halick, Bill Heinrich, Kevin Henley, Mark Hodgins, Hanna Kielar, Ashton Keys, Ben Lauren, Libby Hoffman, Christopher Irvin, Keesa Johnson, Erin Kendricks, Jess Knott, Becky Matz, Melissa McDaniels, Mike McLeod, Nick Noel, Dawn Opel, Abby Rubley, Heather Shea, Maddie Shellgren, Sarah Schultz, Erin VanSloten, Blythe White, Kenny Williams Jr., and Ryan Yang. It has been a pleasure to work with people who are genuinely interested and eager to test new ideas, new processes, and new ways of thinking.

We would like to acknowledge those who contributed to the creation and completion of this book: Courtney Schwabe, for the Hub Design process graphics; Erica Venton and Robynn Verhaeghe, for designing graphs for specific projects; and finally, our thanks to Greg Britton and his team at Johns Hopkins University Press, as well as the reviewers of the manuscript, for their enthusiasm for the project, the pace at which we were able to work, and the insightful and challenging suggestions for revision.

We also owe an enormous debt of gratitude to those who have been thought partners in this work. Leigh Graves Wolf was key to bringing the idea of the Hub from one-pager to reality. Mark Sullivan was part of that first committee of faculty and has long proven himself to be one of the boldest voices for a vision of higher education focused on helping people become their fullest, most creative selves. Sekhar Chivukula and Mark Largent, in their time as associate provost for Undergraduate Education, have been creative and courageous partners. We have been happy to follow their lead. As individuals, each has been a generous and supportive colleague. Karen Klomparens, who helped found MSU's graduate school and understands academic startups, has been a wise mentor and guide. We also were fortunate to have a provost, June Youatt, who could see around corners, genuinely cares about students, is creative, and who understood early on the need for faculty and students to author their own innovations.

As these acknowledgments show, this project has been a large-scale effort and a joyous one, at that.

Design for Change in Higher Education

Designing Change in Higher Education

We can and should design the next iteration of higher education.

There are all sorts of fun questions and tensions embedded in that sentence. Can higher education institutions change? History shows us they do, but can they do so reasonably quickly? Can higher education change in response to needs that move faster than the time it took to develop the modern research university? Then there is the ethical imperative in *should*. Why should we? And who gets to decide? Which brings us to *we*. Who counts? Higher education institutions are designed to be exclusive and hierarchical, which means that there are significant limitations on who gets to participate in deciding the good, the true, and the beautiful when it comes to higher education.

There is no question that higher education in the United States faces significant challenges. An October 22, 2019, *Inside Higher Education* story does a succinct job identifying those challenges based on survey results from the American Council on Education, Huron Consulting Group, and the Georgia Institute of Technology.[1] The list includes our lack of preparedness for issues like demographic change, the continued defunding of public education, cost pressures for both public and private institutions, and the opportunities and challenges presented by educational technologies.

Add to that list the shock of the COVID-19 pandemic, which will reverberate for years.

Given the contexts of US higher education, there should be a premium placed on change functions—on creativity, innovation, and change management. For some, the desire for a change function would be driven by identifying opportunities. For others, it would be driven by a recognition that institutions will be forced to change in the near future. If these statements about the challenges to higher education and the need to adapt are correct (or at least plausible), it is surprising how few institutions have functions focused on thoughtful, iterative problem-solving and opportunity identification.

This book is about the power and importance of design to the project of transforming higher education. We imagine our audience to be quite broad, because we believe that the stakeholders and participants in the project of reimagining higher education are also broad. Faculty are essential, of course, and students are fundamental. Staff are often ignored in conversations about higher education and that is a problem—particularly given that some of the authors of this book are academic staff and important voices at our university. Little of what we imagine in these pages is possible without strong, courageous, and progressive academic leadership, from the department to governing boards. We hope that each of these audiences finds something valuable in what we offer.

We hope that the arguments we make here will foster an ongoing conversation. We believe that design is a transformative process, and we also believe that higher education institutions should embrace design as a pathway for facilitating necessary changes. We offer the story of the Hub for Innovation in Learning and Technology at Michigan State University (MSU) as an argument, as well. The Hub is an internal design consultancy, and while there are a number of innovation hubs and groups around higher education, our version is somewhat unusual. The Hub as it exists at Michigan State might not be the answer everywhere, but we believe something like the Hub is necessary in many places.

Herbert Simon famously argued that design is the core activity of the professions, and we are going to take that argument seriously in exploring the extent to which design practice is a core competency of the university. We hope that our perspective and design stance inspires others to think with us. We know some will disagree with what we offer, and we welcome that. Our goal is to help others think, explore, and create. To start, this introduction will work through a number of issues that contextualize the rest of the book: our take on the possibilities of institutional change, our stance with regard to the concept and practice of *design*, and the origin story of the Hub.

Higher Education Is More Agile Than Most People Think

Higher education faces significant challenges, and there are plenty of ideas about how to address them. In her 2017 book, for example, Cathy Davidson calls for a complete redesign of higher education around a "new education" that is "ethical, democratic, pragmatic . . . that not only uses technology wisely and creatively but also understands its limits and its impacts and addresses its failings."[2] Her vision is echoed by scholars William Moner, Phillip Motley, and Rebecca Pope-Ruark, who see an acute historical need for higher education to be "redesigned in both its approaches and the structure of its institutions to more vibrantly prepare students to be bold, empathetic, community-oriented citizens who can both frame and address the complex societal problems in the future."[3] Still others, such as William Bowen and Michael McPherson, insist that educational attainment rates must increase and that institutions must become much more effective, particularly with regard to teaching, learning, and related educational outcomes.[4]

Such proposals seem impossible given the commonplace assumption that universities haven't—and cannot—change. Yet that assumption isn't true. As Davidson notes, "the modern American university is only about 150 years old ... the infrastructure, curriculum, and assessment methods we have now were developed between 1860 and 1925."[5] Her claim is supported by David Labaree's history of American higher education, which tells the story of a loose, relatively autonomous, and entrepreneurial system capable of seeking and creating markets and adapting to circumstances. His book begins with what we think is a remarkable paragraph:

> The American system of higher education is an anomaly. In the twentieth century it surged past its European forebears to become the dominant system in the world—with more money, talent, scholarly esteem, and institutional influence than any of the systems that served as its models. By all rights, this never should have happened. Its origins were remarkably humble: a loose assortment of parochial nineteenth-century liberal arts colleges, which emerged in the pursuit of sectarian expansion and civic boosterism more than scholarly distinction. These colleges had no academic credibility, no reliable source of students, and no steady funding. Yet these weaknesses of the American system in the nineteenth century turned out to be strengths in the twentieth. In the absence of strong funding and central control, individual colleges had to learn how to survive and thrive in a highly competitive market, in which they needed to rely on student tuition and alumni donations and had to develop a mode of governance that would position them to pursue any opportunity and cultivate any source of patronage. As a result, American colleges developed into an emergent system of higher education that was lean, adaptable, autonomous, consumer sensitive, self-supporting, and radically decentralized.[6]

What enabled the American (un)system to develop is a mix of macro-level factors, many having little to do with education: the emergence of the United States as an economic and military power, the dominance of English as a global language, the destruction of European universities in two wars, and the related growth and investment in US higher education during and after those wars. Labaree argues that the lack of centralized support for US higher education, with few church or state ties, meant that institutions had more autonomy to organize themselves internally and to pursue external opportunities, including the ability to "expand access and increase scholarly quality at the same time."[7] It is also true that the lack of central authority means that there is very little system to speak of.

This dynamic has produced its share of problems as well. US higher education is highly stratified, with a number of social and institutional problems. Perhaps most familiar is Labaree's claim that American higher education "allows the successes of the research university to occur at the expense of the students attending the community college and regional state university. In many ways, the top American universities are so rich and so academically distinguished largely because the institutions at the bottom are so poor and so undistinguished."[8]

Regardless, what emerges from the history of US higher education is not precisely the battleship that is difficult to turn but something more dynamic and innovative. As Adrianna Kezar notes, "significant changes have occurred throughout the history of higher education."[9] She goes on to note signature moments such as the Yale Report of 1928; the Morrill Act, which gave us the land-grant institution (1862); and the GI Bill after the Second World War. She notes as well, however, that each of her examples is an instance of "pressure" from the outside that resulted in change. There are fewer examples of changes that are internally motivated. Yet when Davidson calls for educators and administrators "committed to redesigning an ethical, democratic, pragmatic, forward-looking education," it is possible to think that we can, in fact, redesign higher education.[10]

Joshua Kim and Edward Maloney also see the potential for change in higher education. They are interested in the implications of what they argue is a "turn to learning" in higher education. They write:

> We have come to believe . . . that new learning programs and initiatives—along with new and reorganized learning centers and units that have emerged over the past few years—need to be understood as part of a larger and more coherent higher education story. We believe that we are in the midst of a higher education-wide shift. This larger trend is animating much of the specific and idiosyncratic campus changes that

we and our colleagues at other colleges and universities are both creating and navigating.[11]

They also recognize the history of adaptation in American higher education, and they see that we are working at a moment in history that is open to change and under tremendous pressure to do so. However, while arguing for this turn to learning and the dynamism it implies, they also "find it curious that how universities go about understanding and designing for learning is so little understood or documented itself."[12] As they note, the literature on learning and what works in education is extensive. What is poorly understood and rarely executed (or even attempted) is how change is facilitated in relation to what we understand. They remind us that "we do not have a comprehensive understanding of how theories of design, technology, innovation, and analytics are challenging our fundamental assumptions about teaching and learning in higher education."[13] A key question of theirs shapes our book: How then do universities change to improve student learning?[14] We build on that to ask a larger question, How do universities change?

If it is necessary to redesign higher education for the near future, how, precisely, can this happen—and happen quickly? How do institutions change? Is it possible for a university to become a design organization? Davidson asks us "to work together to rejuvenate an antiquated system for our accelerating times and to ensure that the solutions we craft address the real problems rather than just generating new ones."[15] To do so requires specific and systemic ways to solve the problems we care about as educators and learners. To do so requires design.

Our argument is that the only way to achieve what Davidson, Bass, Kim, Maloney, and others advocate is through design, and more specifically, for colleges and universities to build design functions as a core capacity. As Kim and Maloney note, "learning innovation is as much about leading organizational change as it is about pedagogy and technology."[16] We think they understate the case: it is all about how to recognize and facilitate organizational change. The key shift, which the Hub was explicitly designed to address, is the move from the individual to the collective, from the classroom to the institution. This move is inclusive of the experiences of specific classrooms and individual teachers and students, but, as Kim and Maloney also note, it relocates "the unit of analysis of the conditions that support or inhibit student learning from that of the individual student to the scale of the institution and everywhere in between."[17]

Institutions "R" Us

If the institution is the unit of interest for design, then this assumes that institutions can change. As Labaree as others have shown, higher education institutions do change, but we don't have a century to work and wait. We need to support changes that happen relatively quickly. But what does it mean to change an institution? Nearly twenty years ago, Jeff and other colleagues began thinking and writing about this question. They took a rhetorical approach to institutional change (their discipline), which claims that, since institutions are fundamentally rhetorical entities, rhetoric can be used to change them. They argued for "institutional critique," which constitutes "a method that insists that institutions, as unchangeable as they may seem (and, indeed, often are), do contain spaces for reflection, resistance, revision, and productive action. This method insists that sometimes individuals (writing teachers, researchers, writers, students, citizens) can rewrite institutions through rhetorical action."[18]

That article names a number of methods that work to identify places where change is possible (in addition to place, there is also an essential element of time, or *kairos*, which signals timeliness and appropriateness of action). Methods include forms of spatial thinking to explore social, disciplinary, and institutional relationships, and in relation to that, boundary interrogation. Our favorite is the identification and use of "zones of ambiguity." These "zones" can

often (but not always) be found within the processes of decision making (people acting through institutions). Again, these processes (rhetorical systems) are the very structure of the institution itself. It is within these processes that people within an institutional space talk, listen, act, and confront differences. We suggest that not only do institutions orchestrate semiotic systems, but that semiotic systems (rhetoric) orchestrate institutions. Thus, institutions are both material and rhetorical spaces, and our definition of them must encompass these elements as well as our sense of spatial scales—our location of institutions at both macro and micro levels. In our case, we seek to change institutions through acts that constitute a critical rhetoric of institutional design.[19]

Thinking such as this has had a significant impact on how we conceptualized, designed, and practiced the Hub. The Hub is a "third space" within the institution, both physically and rhetorically. It is designed to be ambiguous in terms of where it fits within MSU's organizational chart, with regard to its (non?)disciplinarity and with regard to how we work. Positioning such as this carries tremendous risk. We are, for example, at constant risk of being unintelligible to others. We are at the edges of any number of boundaries, but that also gives us a certain amount of rhetorical agency within the institution. Readers of the argument that Kim and Maloney lay out in *Learning Innovation* will recognize the fragility of the Hub as an organization. At this point in our development and in the development of analogous organizations, fragility is inevitable. But, as we hope to lay out in this book, the fundamental design stance and practice of the Hub is a solution for identifying, developing, and sustaining learning innovations.

The institutional critique framework is useful for understanding why some of the specific projects the Hub supports seem to be working to push the institution, and just as importantly, why we choose to work on certain projects and not others. The simple math for us is this: the right project portfolio + execution = a changed institution. "Right" means that the project has significant impact, is an exciting model for campus, or aligns with stakeholder priorities. But "right" also means that the project changes key processes of decision-making and institutional practice such that the students, faculty, departments, or the programs that own and must sustain the project will not be the same again. There isn't much bling or glory in this stance. It isn't about "innovative" or "transformative" technologies. Institutional change is simply hard work, animated by imagination, but driven by careful design (rhetorical) practice.

If we believe that we can and should design the next iteration of higher education, then we also must believe that we are the authors of our institutions; "We made 'em, we can fix 'em. Institutions R Us."[20] The challenging problem is how, of course, and there is no shortage of strategies, techniques, and tips on offer. It is design that changes the relationship between theory and action, a change that is required if we are to make elegant and effective transitions (and translations) between ideas of what higher education should be in any given instance and the materiality of those ideas.

A Design Stance for Higher Education

Design can and does mean any number of things. Our take on the concept of design clearly shapes how we operate. The term names an area of expert practice and indexes more than one academic field or discipline. We inherit a notion of design as an exclusively expert activity that is primarily associated with art or product development or engineering. While true, design is now widely distributed and participatory, largely because design has become a powerful way to conceptualize and address problems and opportunities. As Ezio Manzini writes, "in a world in rapid and profound transformation, we are all designers."[21] In this respect, design is what Manzini characterizes as "a way of thinking and doing things that entails reflection and strategic sense, that calls us to look at ourselves and our context and decide whether and how to act to improve the state of things."[22] Richard Buchanan notes that design deals "with matters of choice, with things that may be other than they are."[23] But thinking and acting in this way isn't easy. Design is a fundamental human capacity *and* requires specific forms of expertise.

A design practice in higher education lives this tension between exclusive and inclusive, between expertise and participation. However, it has not been our experience that the practice of design is widely distributed in higher education. Quite the opposite. But it has been our experience that the *need* and *desire* to design exists in our institutions—from academics to residential and hospitality services to student affairs to buildings and grounds. And not surprisingly, there is tremendous expertise and capacity within a university for design. For a design group inside higher education like the Hub for Innovation in Learning and Technology, therefore, there are significant affordances for design. However, there are few conceptual or practical models.

We've been searching for a design language that is both conceptually rich and also enables a specific design practice. We wanted a vernacular that has clear space for expertise and is also accessible to everyone. Our choices in this book reflect our stance on design and frame our design practice at the Hub and in higher education. Our practice is grounded in the ancient design arts of rhetoric and expands from there. For our purposes here, we might characterize rhetoric as the art of changing the world through language. More concretely, our practice is concentrated on facilitating the right sorts of conversations about learning and education. *Conversation*, in this case, is a term of art fundamental to design. Paul Pangero writes that "design is grounded in argumentation, and therefore requires conversation, so that participants may understand, agree, and collaborate, all toward effective action."[24] Pangero's design theory is grounded in "second order" cybernetics, or what Pangero calls the science of effective action: "an ethical, clear-eyed argument for transparent, value-driven design processes."[25] For our purposes here, Pangero's cybernetics and our take on rhetoric help create a shared understanding of "conversations" as having conceptual and practical value.

We are committed to helping people act well in the world. We are grounded in language practices, in conversation (*dialogue*, in rhetorical theory). We have well-established analytical stances and practices and are necessarily concerned with ethics, politics, and power. Conversation is related to argumentation and to understanding, with the goal of some agreements and collaboration (action is quite difficult without agreement—ethical action likely impossible). We see design itself as a type of conversation, and our practice is focused on designing conversations as a participatory mode of identifying and realizing opportunities.

The present moment for higher education requires more than a participatory design stance, however. The pandemic has deepened inequalities. We see, for instance, communities, schools, and students historically excluded from the best of what our education system has to offer struggling yet again with fewer resources to "pivot" their educational practices. Like many, we are disgusted and deeply saddened by the deaths of Breonna Taylor, George Floyd, Manuel Ellis, and so many more. These deaths are not isolated incidences but instead are linked in a terrible chain of anti-Black, white supremacist policies and actions by institutions—including institutions of higher education— that go back hundreds of years.

As our colleague Mark Largent has highlighted, Michigan State is full of what he calls "low bridges": policies, practices, and cultures that were accidentally or intentionally designed to keep people from succeeding. This focus on the institution, on what some call the "context" in which students and educators work, is essential. Beronda Montgomery says this most clearly and forcefully with reference to the context of mentoring:

> primarily white or majority institutions commonly adopt individual-deficit mentoring models in attempting to "support" individuals in adapting to academic environments, particularly in regards to minoritized or underrepresented students and faculty . . . Less frequently do institutions attempt to investigate or assess the effects of prevailing and commonly accepted biases, institutional cultures, or structural barriers, such as racism, sexism, or classism, present in academic environments in which students or faculty exhibit challenges progressing towards intended individual outcomes. Culture-centered or barrier-mediating interventions depend upon surveying environments comprehensively

and initiating active efforts to position institutions to address barriers across entire ecosystems, not just defaulting to a unilateral focus on fixing individual-related concerns.[26]

A design stance relevant for this moment, then, must address these facts. Design is not neutral. Therefore, attention to who participates in conversations, when those conversations happen, and the values and sensibilities that inform our practices are fundamental concerns. This requires the design of equitable processes, which include analytical and sense-making moments, and of course, equity as we iterate and implement.

As a design pattern, a "conversation" has some common elements:

1. Identifying participants in a way that is inclusive and privileges those most impacted
2. Committing to ideation that is attentive to perspective, difference, and turn-taking
3. Analyzing our shared discourse
4. Prototyping and iterating based on feedback
5. Understanding and committing to action

There is one final point that reinforces the importance of *conversation* as a design practice: it is grounded in language. Most universities are, quite literally, a universe of perspectives, disciplines, and values, all indexed by language. We cannot assume, for example, that *critique*, as used here, while highly valued in the humanities, will have the same meaning and value for our colleagues from other parts of the known intellectual universe. We need to be in conversation with each other to understand each other.

Our design stance, therefore, is grounded in conversations that become ways to conceptualize problems and opportunities to discover (research) and invent (make) the means by which a group of people come to a shared understanding about what should exist with regard to learning, education, and the future of our university. This stance enables efforts to frame how design might proceed inside a higher education institution.

Design Functions and Organizations:
The Hub for Innovation in Learning and Technology

Like many things, the Hub began as a single sheet of paper. An idea. Michigan State University's provost at the time was convinced that the university needed a "third space" on campus, one that would invite a new type of thinking. That space needed to be cultural, intellectual, and physical, and it needed to facilitate creativity with direction. That is, the work of this new place needed to produce outcomes. Why? Because this provost knew the challenges facing Michigan State—many of the challenges we identify in this introduction—and was interested in coming up with answers to the question, What sort of educational institution does MSU need to become in order to meet our mission in the near future? This new function was also intended to support the university's student success initiative. MSU is still engaged in a project to increase its overall graduation rate and close opportunity gaps for specific populations of students (e.g., minoritized groups). These two rationales were linked. We need to reinvent ourselves as a learning institution because that is the only way we are going to address our most pressing student challenge: graduating everyone we admit, regardless of circumstance.

In some respects, the origin of the Hub is a much earlier version of an argument that Steven Mintz makes in *Inside Higher Education*, namely, that higher education needs "centers for educational innovation, evaluation and research" to meet the acute needs of the sector.[27] Mintz's frame of reference is adapting centers for teaching and learning for this purpose, which is certainly one pathway (we have had many conversations with directors of such centers over the past four years). The need, as Mintz sees it, is to address the structural weaknesses with those centers, given the challenges that need to be addressed. Mintz argues that the services of most teaching and learning centers are "voluntary, and [that] staff found it difficult to reach beyond the usual suspects, typically a subset of junior faculty and graduate students." He goes on to write that most centers "existed in a silo and weren't empowered to drive academic transformation. Indeed, most lack the expertise to inform institutional strategies involving learning assessment or software and technology acquisition, let alone online programming." Given the challenges of the present moment, the structure, agency, and culture around teaching and learning functions in higher education are inadequate.

We believe that Mintz is correct. It matters little to us if a university creates a new function (like the Hub) or repurposes an existing function (a teaching and learning center). What matters much more is the responsibility, agency, and resources given to this innovation function, and, as we argue in this book, its mission (transformation, not service) and approach (design). The committee of faculty who moved from a one-pager to a proposal that MSU create the Hub spent a great deal of time worrying about the tension between "innovation" and "service." Some warned that the burdens of service would consume all capacity to be creative and warned as well that the power dynamics of the university were such that, without a clear mandate to push the edges, the activity of this imagined Hub for Innovation would become normalized to incremental improvements to the status quo. Questions of *how* to move people from the current state of affairs to a new, better state were foremost in the minds of this committee. "Create the Hub," they said, and start worrying right away about how to help faculty and students innovate.

The provost created the Hub, which was both a startup (new function and culture) and a realignment (of existing people). Our first design project was the Hub itself, focused on identity, culture, and behavior (practice), a design project that continues to the present day. We began quickly, working on an initial set of projects almost immediately. We partnered with an architectural firm to design a workspace that was intended to facilitate project-based collaborations with partners from across campus. That space doesn't look much different from many "open" office plans outside higher education, but it is a unique workplace inside the university. We will discuss later in this book the role that this literal "third space" plays in facilitating process and outcomes. Most importantly, we worked on *projects*, and this is a feature that is so mundane that it can easily become invisible. The Hub is a project-based organization. We are what we do. That portfolio of work constitutes our identity and how we are measured, but it also has been part of our answer for *how* we will privilege innovation over service. We have some agency to choose to work on efforts, brought to us by faculty, students, staff, and leadership, that promise to be transformative. We add capacity to those projects, and if successful, help our colleagues transition the outcomes of our work together back into their domains as positive and sustainable changes. Perhaps most importantly, as we worked our way through our startup year and succeeded and failed with our initial portfolio, we realized quickly that success required us to build a design practice that was habituated to the cultures and practices of higher education. We needed to become a design organization, which is the intellectual and practical project described in this book.

Indeed, to do the work imagined in this book requires a design organization. We mean that in two senses: (1) the creation of a design organization inside universities, and ideally (2) the university itself as a design organization. A design organization in the broadest sense is organized around human beings and what they need to be better, happier, and so on. Disney, for example, designs for "happiness." It's worthwhile to consider what your university designs for. In this regard, educational institutions have built-in advantages with respect to being driven by values. Almost everyone can agree, for example, that universities exist to help students and their broader communities learn. They also exist to discover good ideas and share them to the benefit of those same communities. Faculty and staff might readily agree that we are focused on high-quality student experiences—in our classes, in living units, as an outcome of our research and creative programs, and so on.

A design organization is important because to redesign higher education requires more than arguments to do so or values that might animate design. It requires cultural and practical capacity that most institutions currently lack. The Hub for Innovation in Learning and Technology is a design group inside a large university, and in this respect, it is a bet that faculty, students, and staff are willing to bring forward ideas for change and engage in design as a way to explore the possibility that our universities can be other than they are. It is also a material argument for a kind of work that must happen in higher education.

The function of a design organization is to support institutional change. As Cooper and Junginger note, any organizational change "is an activity that cannot be accomplished without organizing or reorganizing people, tasks, structures and resources in such a way that they align" with a story of hopes and aspirations in that organization.[28] This is a complex matrix of work that is particularly daunting in university organizations, which are still remarkably medieval in their organization. Yet universities share many characteristics of large institutions where change is incremental at best and "change management" largely nonexistent as a practice. In this book, we argue for design as the most effective and creative approach to change management. As Meyer notes, many organizations "often find themselves locked into a mechanistic operational mode and undifferentiated in the marketplace . . . [and] are often unsure about how to identify and act upon growth opportunities, and may have even set up systems and structures that actively work against new value creation."[29] Meyer puts the issue more strongly: "Organizations send out antibodies to fight and reject new approaches, and this is what design must contend with when it enters an organization."[30] While many academics will resist the market language here, this description of organizational life should ring true. The value of design for an organization is its ability to help people imagine and create possibilities.

The value of a design function within a higher education organization is its presence as a cultural, intellectual, and ideally, physical space for faculty and students to work across boundaries, systems, and structures. In many respects, however, the processes and practices of design are just as valuable as the "products." This is what Meyer calls the "intrinsic value of design," which includes the many influences and outcomes that result from engaging customers, employees, and organizational dynamics in the design process. In other words, value is "inherent in the means, rather than the ends. Such values include social cohesion, ideological coherence, and strategic alignment that emerge from participation in design activities."[31] This value is only possible if design is participatory, if design is a core activity of the university, and if it is expertly facilitated and led. As Meyer also notes, the "key to capturing the intrinsic side of the equation . . . is to understand design as a set of activities: methods, approaches, and techniques that provide its practitioners with a way of working together in a highly productive way."[32] What is required is expertise and experience in design processes and activities, in analysis, research, and assessment, and in the change management work required to enact participatory and inclusive institutional critique and change.

We can and should design the next iteration of higher education, and we must do it in ways that are thoughtful, sustainable, and not necessarily "disruptive," which carries so many deserved negative connotations. And while there are "hubs" and "innovation" groups all over higher education, without a design theory and practice that is developed inside higher education and grounded in the contexts and cultures of education, we fear that most efforts will fall short. If the challenges facing us are as grave as the literature and current events suggest, then the biggest challenge is the extent to which we are capable of asking and answering fundamental questions about our purpose as institutions and then aligning our work with those purposes. To ask and answer questions like these is to design. The ability to become a design organization might determine if higher education in the United States is still capable of seeking and creating opportunities and adapting to circumstances, as Labaree suggests we historically have been.

Equity as Innovation

We write this book not just during a pandemic but also during a period of uprising. We've noted the importance of equity to our design stance, but we believe that issues of equity also represent significant opportunities for innovation. One of the reasons the Hub exists is to support a wide-ranging strategic focus of the university intended to eliminate persistent opportunity gaps for first-generation students and students of color. From inception, therefore, we have seen issues of equity not simply as a moral imperative but also as an innovation priority. Rarely does equity appear in the popular or scholarly work on innovation in any sector, let alone higher education. But we see many of the needed changes in higher education in terms of equity.

Seeing equity as a space for innovation begins with recognizing our own implication and participation in an educational system that contributes to the inequalities we see in our daily lives and that are reflected in the news that appears on our screens. It continues by acknowledging that the learning experience design (LXD) methodologies we utilize are themselves embedded within paradigms that carry both privilege and oppression. We understand that it is our duty to question, critique, and champion participatory design practices that will, in turn, impact student, staff, and faculty success on our campus equitably. To promote equity in our design strategy, we are committed to practicing inclusion in our design activities, increasing diversity in our design processes, and advocating for social justice in our design collaborations. Given the collaborative nature of our work, commitments such as these are challenging to live out, but if done well, will result in a number of changes in our own institution that will make us more equitable educators. Those changes will indeed be innovative.

Consider MSU's student success initiative, which is animated both by the belief that all our students have the ability to learn, persist, and succeed and by the commitment to create equitable pathways that enable students to do so. The key outcomes of our student success initiative focus on increasing our overall graduation rate and closing persistent fifteen-point gaps for specific student populations.[33] To achieve these goals requires a comprehensive approach to the academic operations of the university—change management at scale (though change management frameworks and practices per se haven't been systematically utilized at MSU—see more in chapter 4).

Our work at MSU is linked to our participation in the University Innovation Alliance (UIA). The UIA focuses on areas of policy and practice that were first developed at either Arizona State University, Georgia State University, or the University of Florida:

- Predictive analytics and data-driven interventions
- Adaptive learning
- Financial interventions
- Precollege or bridge programs
- Targeted student success supports that reach out to specific subgroups of students

Even this list suggests significant potential for academic innovation and change in higher education, and again, each of these is focused on equity. Michigan State's work streams have included areas of practice such as proactive advising, which focuses on activities that help advisors support students through direct interaction; student-centered process reviews, which seek to identify and change institutional processes that affect student success; and one of our key contributions to US higher education, our Neighborhoods concept, which was a complete redesign of our approach to housing and its relationship to student affairs.

Yet arguably the most important and difficult student success issues are those that touch curriculum and instruction. We believe more equitable learning experiences are foundational to a more equitable university. This is precisely where the Hub fits into this larger strategic landscape. What the example of the student success initiative suggests is how much opportunity exists for change in higher education animated by a commitment to equity. Innovation and change most often focuses on technology and new approaches to education, such as online programs and new credentials. Living up to our moral and ethical obligations to meet our students where they are and to help them achieve their dreams would be one heck of an innovation.

Overview of the Remainder of the Book

This is the "book" part of a playbook. The book is more conceptual than our design plays, which are available at http://hubplaybook.org.

In the book, we articulate the ideas behind our work. Each chapter is structured around a case example (or two) intended to ground and complicate the ideas on offer. Our ideas form a design stance and describe a practice that draws from a variety of intellectual traditions and practical experiences. On the website, readers will find plays that we have developed along with our adaptations of the plays of others. Some will like the plays more than the book because the plays are concrete, actionable, and (re)usable. Yet we have found theory to be the most practical tool for our work, and we hope that this book will also be experienced as concrete, actionable, and (re)usable.

The book unfolds in the following way. In our first chapter, we begin with learning experience design (LXD) and two claims that are important for our larger argument. First, LXD names an increasingly critical practice and a new type of academic professional. These professionals sit at the heart of design and change in higher education. Second, we believe the focus of design in higher education should be the "experience." Our focus on experience is critical to our design stance and cascades across the chapters of the book.

Chapter 2 deepens and extends our approach to LXD by putting design, systems, and future thinking in relation to one another. We also discuss the roots of our design practice, which incorporates a number of familiar elements from the design world and remixes them in ways suited to address the challenges of higher education. To bring together our LXD design practice more concretely, we explore the case of the development of the iOS Design Lab, which is unique to MSU as an experiential learning opportunity open to all students.

When asked what we most commonly design, our answer is *conversations*. The "conversation," for us, is both metaphorical and concrete. Conversation is core to our work because the practice of conversation allows us to make thinking visible and to build awareness about the contexts in which change is being imagined. Designed conversations slow down institutionalized routines, break down silos, and create momentum around our thoughts, attitudes, intentions, and resistance to change. In chapter 3 we focus on design conversations and propose that the way we design for conversations about learning experiences is crucial in encouraging innovation in higher education. To illustrate, we walk through the example of the French program's curriculum redesign. This chapter is concerned with describing design conversations as tools for change and positions the learning experience designer as change facilitator.

Chapter 4 argues for understanding change management as design. We argue for moving the language around change in higher education from one of "management" to "design" because such a move opens new and expanded possibilities for participatory change. We also believe that the most effective and sustainable changes in higher education will come as outcomes of design inquiries. One issue that has become clear to us is that all of our projects are change management projects, but change management isn't a commonly used approach by most academic programs. Conversely, few change management processes are applied to the academic functions of higher education. To illustrate the complexity of learning design and change management, we provide the complicated case of a large-scale curriculum reform in our College of Veterinary Medicine. We made a number of useful mistakes in that project, and we believe that the example (and chapter) illustrates that the most meaningful organizational changes happen on the way to something else.

Chapter 5 is written by two of our colleagues, Bill Heinrich and Becky Matz, and focuses on the role of assessment and research in a design organization. The chapter argues that design should be grounded in assessment and research, from assessment of innovative designs that inform decision-making to the production of scholarly work that contributes to a research domain. Our colleagues describe approaches to assessment and research that are useful for conceptualizing problems and creating opportunities for change. In an organization like the Hub, which is focused on transformation in an institution that values and rewards research, these activities have additional symbolic value by providing ways for partners to develop relationships based on accountability. Becky and Bill walk readers through a number of examples where either assessment or research was critical to design, such as mathematics reform and the development of a learning analytics practice. The key takeaway is that assessment and research are vital to a design agenda that seeks to be transformative.

In our sixth and final chapter, we deal with building a design organization. It was clear early in our start-up phase that to be effective, we needed to build a design organization to enable our practice. Taking up the mantra from our early days that "the first project of the Hub is the Hub," this chapter describes the principles and practices that guided the design of the organization itself by way of a concrete focus on DesignOps and the professional development program we built to support individual and collective growth. DesignOps has largely gained traction over the last five years as companies are growing their design practices. It names those processes and programs that support high-quality methods and how an organization organizes tools, workflow, and people for smooth outcomes. There is no sustainable design in higher education without a design organization, and this chapter is a starting place for how to build one appropriate for the contexts of colleges and universities.

1

Learning Experience Design
in Higher Education

WITH THE INTRODUCTION providing the historical and institutional context for our work, this chapter is shaped by two claims that are important for the larger argument of the book. First, learning experience design (LXD) names an increasingly critical practice in higher education. It also names a new type of academic professional, one who sits at the heart of design and change in higher education. Second, we believe the focus of design in higher education should be experience. These two claims suggest an even more important idea: the university itself is a designed experience (or set of more or less intentionally designed experiences), and any effort to reimagine higher education needs to begin with this idea. Every college or university provides students with a set of intentional learning experiences inside and outside the classroom, and all these experiences are within the boundaries of learning experience design.

One recent way into the conversation about LXD is the 2016 MIT Online Education Policy Initiative report, which argues for creating the role of the "learning engineer" in higher education, or what Martin Smith describes as "people with terminal degrees in traditional academic disciplines who also have experience with design and interdisciplinary collaboration and an appetite for bleeding-edge technology" (the notion of a learning engineer goes back at least to Herbert Simon).[1] The MIT report expands: "Learning engineers must have a knowledge base in the learning sciences, familiarity with modern education technology, and an understanding of and practice with design principles. Preferably, they will also have a deep grounding in a specific discipline such as physics, biology, engineering, history, or music."[2]

The focus on learning sciences and disciplinary knowledge is important, as is the focus on design. Fortunately, we have decades of scholarly and practical work on university campuses in the scholarship of teaching and learning, which has built necessary expertise. Importantly, the National Research Council has underlined the need for developing and valuing disciplinary educational expertise. As they note in their report on discipline-based educational research (DBER), "DBER investigates learning and teaching in a discipline using a range of methods with deep grounding in the discipline's priorities, worldview, knowledge, and practices. It is informed by and complementary to more general research on human learning and cognition."[3] To achieve the goals of transforming learning in the sciences, in other words, educational practices and learning design require expert disciplinary knowledge. Fortunately, such knowledge is easy to find on most university campuses. The work is to ensure that learning design is informed by it.

Conversations about new roles in higher education, like that of the learning engineer, recognize a need to develop new sorts of academic professionals who have both the domain expertise and the understanding of the university's organizational culture to serve a critical function for higher education. We see our work and stance as consistent with these conversations but with a shift from engineering to design (which isn't necessarily a big shift). The more substantial shift is to "experience" and what that means for the truly remarkable scope for experience design in higher education. Before we get there, however, we think it is important to engage the existing conversation on learning design because it will help to trace the conceptual shift that we believe could be transformative.

In doing so, we are really not interested in definitional issues (e.g., what is *learning design?*) or contrasts with related or overlapping design professions (e.g., instructional design).[4] Definitional and professional boundaries are simply not helpful at this moment. We need a big tent. We *are* very much interested in the conceptual shift from "instruction" to "learning" because it allows us to get to experience. Finally, and relatedly, we argue for an expansion in the domains in which learning experience design must work.

Designing Experiences to Support Learning

The purpose of this section is to come to terms with terms. In our own design practice, we wrestle with terms because they index professional identities as much as they name professional practices. These terms constitute a field of argument, one that we share with a number of colleagues practicing learning experience design across higher education.[5]

In most tellings, learning (experience) design (LD or LXD) emerged from a prior notion of instructional design, which has its own history and field of application—primarily in the design of online courses and programs, but with new layers added from design practices that first emerged outside of higher education. Soulis, Seitzinger, and Nicolettou argue that "learner experience design (sometimes learning experience design) is an emerging approach to learning design that uses methods borrowed from related design disciplines such as user experience design and service design thinking"[6] Or as Whitney Kilgore describes this emergence:

> Instructional designers, like web developers in the '90s, historically had expertise in conveying content through a limited set of tools and platforms, such as a learning management system (LMS). LX designers, in contrast, merge design-thinking principles with curriculum development and the application of emerging technologies to help faculty tailor content to student behaviors and preferences. It cuts across disciplines and moves beyond the LMS: LX designers embrace graphic design,

multimedia production, research-based standards and social media. They are partners to faculty throughout the program and course development process.[7]

Indeed, as Soulis, Seitzinger, and Nicolettou continue, LXD often needs "to orchestrate the design for products (such as learning resources), systems (such as a course shell in a learning management system) and services (such as timely feedback or discussion facilitation)."[8] The picture of the profession that has emerged, as the *Horizon Report* characterizes it, is one in which

> the instructional design role has seen growth and professional recognition beyond standard course design and development. Additional responsibilities such as project management, learning analytics, educational research, faculty mentorship and collaboration, and more academic autonomy have elevated the professional identities and expertise of instructional designers. New methods, processes, and scholarly work are emerging from teaching, learning, and technology communities, introducing new pathways and titles such as learning experience designer (LXD) and learning engineer. Many of these roles are well situated to be high-impact agents of change at their institutions, as they embody and promote student-centered and inclusive mindsets in their collaborations with faculty, students, and staff.[9]

This is a serviceable story of how learning design and learning experience design emerge from instructional design. Again, instructional design's relationship to learning experience design is interesting to us not because one is better or more advanced than another. We are not telling a developmental story here. Far from it. We are interested in what this story tells us about changing values in education and the emergent role of design.

The best way to see changes in value and focus is in the scholarly discourse that seeks to articulate an area of research and theory. In this version of the conversation, learning design is a new field in education that "seeks to develop a descriptive framework for teaching and learning activities . . . and to explore how this framework can assist educators to share and adopt great teaching ideas."[10] Research focused on developing such a descriptive framework is necessary to address the core practical problem "that teachers need support and guidance to make pedagogically informed design decisions to make appropriate use of technologies."[11] The work of Dalziel and others in this volume tell a story of a field of research, and the frameworks presented describe (at a very high level) pedagogical moves, practices, and sequences intended to be applicable to any educational activity. The designs that result are understood to be reusable and shareable patterns, applicable in any number of circumstances: a "pedagogical meta-model."[12]

There are two significant implications from the fact that a field such as this emerges from a practical need in education. First, as Dobozy and Campbell remind us, the research responds to a real need to support "learning designers and educational researchers and educators to document their design decisions and share their learning designs with the wider education community."[13] As we argue in this book, there is no design without research. Second, there is a clear shift via the research field from an inherited notion of (instructional) design focused on content delivery to an interest in more general patterns concerned with activity (e.g., pedagogical moves and practices) and the particularities of educational contexts (and the needed supports in those contexts). As Diana Laurilland argues, "we can only design the means by which there is a good chance that learning will take place."[14] We see in this disciplinary approach to learning design the intention to move from "instruction" to "learning" and toward a more developed design discourse appropriate for education.

The result of both practical and research conversations is a dynamic area of research and practice. We see emergent in higher education a field that "is rapidly evolving through the influence of design thinking, user experience (UX) methods, systems design, advances in the learning sciences, and the emergence of learning analytics."[15] Consider figure 1.1, from the Dutch learning experience designer Niels Floor. As with all emergent ideas, learning experience design pulls

Figure 1.1. The World of Experience Design.
Source: Dutch learning experience designer Niels Floor

from a number of existing practices, professional fields, and scholarly foundations. Many who read this will be able to locate themselves on a map like this—and add to it—but the radical space of this map is the center. Wendt writes, experience design is "the collective activities of multiple design practices including, but not limited to, design research, interaction design, visual design, industrial design, interface design, (information) architecture . . . concerned with the cumulative experiential qualities a user might have with a system, and therefore has its roots in psychology, cognitive sciences, anthropology, sociology, and philosophy, among others."[16]

For a design organization like the Hub for Innovation in Learning and Technology, this expanded language, diverse set of related practices, and multiple professional identities have been foundational. Our scope is much larger than online education or the course itself. Yes, we are interested in the moves that instructors and other educators make to support instruction, but fundamentally, we have shifted our focus toward students and their learning as of preferential interest and the entirety of the university experience as our context. Our contextual commitments are to the experience. In this way, we see the emergence of LXD as intellectually critical to create an expansive design practice for higher education.

Our insistence that learning design focus on experience is an argument, of course. To design from experience and toward (and for) new experiences introduces ideas into learning design practice and significantly expands where learning design can be applied. Our interest in experience builds on developments in learning design identified above, but we want to nudge practice beyond "user experience" (though remain inclusive of it) and beyond the typical product-focused interests of product designers (yet we do like commitments to outcomes like "joy" and any number of affective outcomes that we can and should value in a learning experience). Our nudge to learning experience design is a deep commitment to human experience in all its social, cultural, affective, embodied, and cognitive richness. Learning experiences at a university, if they are to be transformative, need to engage humans in ways that engage purpose and meaning. We cannot think and learn without feeling and connecting.[17] Therefore, our learning design practice entails a commitment to the cultural methods and tactics of the humanities and social sciences.

To illustrate what such a commitment looks like, we take a deep dive into the ideas of Christian Madsbjerg and Mikkel Rasmussen. Their ideas serve as a foundation for our orientation to the concept of experience. Madsbjerg and Rasmussen, in their book *The Moment of Clarity*, tell the story of a digital camera company trying to understand bewildering changes in how young people (and then many of us) used photos, a change that led to a significant decline in market share for their cameras. They could have approached the problem more traditionally (How do we recapture market share?). Instead, they chose to go deep into human behavior: "What [the company] found—digital photography is a form of live theatre for the youth culture—was so much richer than something it might have come up with at a strategy session. Business implications followed organically: design cameras with easy tools for uploading directly to sites, and assume that because most photographs serve as a kind of fluid memory bank for users, make the search functions intuitive and allow them to quickly determine which photos will be permanent and which will be forgotten."[18]

For Madsbjerg and Rasmussen, it has become clear that "management science can tell you how many premium cups of coffee the average American drinks in a day, but phenomenology will help you understand what constitutes the experience of really good coffee."[19] Now, we have no intention of turning everyone into phenomenologists (we aren't), but dwelling with experience—"getting people right" in Madsbjerg and Rasmussen's formulation—is worthwhile.

Madsbjerg and Rasmussen are committed to what they call "sensemaking," or the study of experiences for the purpose of moving from the ordinary and subjective to patterns of understanding that can inform decisions. Their thinking has helped us move from *properties* (e.g., male/female) to *aspects*, where meaning resides. For example, What does it mean to be an African American student on Michigan State University's campus? What difference, if any, does it make if the student is from Detroit or elsewhere? What are the intersectional issues of concern for students? Understanding experience is the only way to get at key aspects of what it means for groups or any given individual to be a student at MSU. Understanding experience and designing to create intentional experiences requires a focus on meaning and relationships (between people, objects, ideas, feelings, and so on). Understanding learning experiences provides design guidance for creating paths to an excellent education. To do so is complex, not simple. To engage in design of this nature deepens and extends what we mean by learning design.

In *Sensemaking*, Madsbjerg unpacks what is introduced in the earlier book. Sensemaking focuses on culture, not individuals; thick data, not thin data; the savannah, not the zoo; creativity, not manufacturing; and the "North Star," not GPS.[20] In our world, for example, we might think in terms of student success, not academic silos. Madsbjerg argues that experience design must leverage sensemaking methods to understand why people believe and act the way they do within the "full complexity and beauty of the lived world."[21] In this way, design is required to understand individuals within quite ordinary and everyday contexts of meaning (culture, thick data, and the savannah). To paraphrase Madsbjerg, unless we know what really matters to students and educators, we can't understand what they need to be effective. Sensemaking is an approach to new ideas that is constructed carefully (but with pace) from specific experiences to more general insights, and in a fashion committed to following paths "filled with twists and turns, dead ends, and unexpected breakthroughs."[22] These messier forms of creativity are possible and powerful if guided by what Madsbjerg calls a *north star*, or a strong sense of purpose that aligns the work with direction and, we would add, passion.

Let's be clear here. The notion of learning experience design we are offering is beyond any technocratic notion of designing instruction or interfaces in an online platform. Such work is important, of course, but the design approach imagined here, while participatory and grounded in human experience, requires expertise (and people) that universities may not have or have organized in a way to engage in this work. Such design work is difficult and likely impossible for faculty to do on their own because they lack all of the necessary expertise. And they certainly lack time. Deep experience design requires an organization committed to design as a normal, if disruptive, way for higher education to function.

The "experience" is the key focus for learning design in higher education for three reasons:

1. It focuses our attention on key contextual issues that impact how students learn and how educators teach.
2. It focuses our attention on people in all of their subjective experiences.
3. It enables us to apply learning design to the entirety of the university's curricular, cocurricular, and extracurricular operations.

In the next section, we walk through an example of what this looks like, helping the university to think of student transitions as an experience.

Experiences of Interest Are beyond the
Course and Classroom

A bundle of learning experiences happen in the time and space from when a student transitions into MSU through their first year. These experiences have a significant impact on student success and well-being. Embedded in this transitions project are courses and related formal learning experiences.

Michigan State University had the opportunity, with the College Transition Project, to create a coherent, student-focused approach to facilitating transitions that increase students' sense of belonging, wellness, and informed decision-making about academic and student life. *The ask* of MSU was to authorize the design of a transitions program that would be expected to address a clear and coherent set of learning and business goals aligned with a clear understanding of the purpose of transitions programming.

More than 8,500 students began their MSU journey in Fall 2019. These students looked forward to MSU preparing them to navigate a world that is increasingly digitized, global, and complex, yet MSU did not have a common collective set of practices to support students' transitions and proactively ensure success for all individuals, particularly from the time of admission to the end of their first year. We created three research nodes—composed of students, faculty, and staff—to consider transitions from the students' perspective, the faculty/research perspective, and the stakeholder/office perspective. Each node focused on core inquiry questions about major first-year milestones, common qualities related to student success, as well as policies, practices, and programs that enhanced or detracted from students' resilience during their transition at MSU.

The inquiry team took a phenomenological approach, with a maximum variation sampling methodology, to document diverse perspectives from individuals and units about their thoughts related to students' transition at MSU, from the time of acceptance through the end of the first year. Teams put emphasis on first-time, full-time students.

To achieve maximum variation sampling, the project coordinators

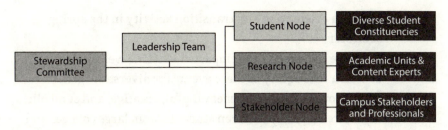

Figure 1.2. Organizational Structure of the Student Transitions Project

created three research nodes composed of students, faculty, and staff to focus on the core inquiry questions from three different lenses: (1) student voices, (2) faculty expertise and research literature, and (3) university offices and initiatives. Finally, the team formed a stewardship group representing units on campus to ensure feedback and insight from as many units and people as possible. Figure 1.2 represents the organization of the transitions project.

As a result of this five-month inquiry, the following recommendations were made for MSU to provide students with transitional experiences that would be future-ready, forward-looking, and focused on their needs:

1. *Develop coherence around the major milestones related to student transition, with an emphasis on high-touch, just-in-time interventions.* Our current practices are decentralized and uncoordinated, with an overemphasis on the start of the year. The impact on students is both overwhelming and incoherent.
   - Create a set of goals and outcomes associated with the first-year transition, map the outcomes to interventions, and ensure consistency and continuity of messaging.
   - Consider all engagement with students and parents as part of transition, create a sense of belonging, and identify specific messages and qualities that should be present at all engagements.
   - Limit the volume of information delivered before arrival on campus and expand welcome period and orientation activities into the fall semester.

- Increase orientation and transition activity in the spring semester.
- Enhance the quality and impact of existing welcome events, as well as the equity of these events for diverse students (make convocation more meaningful, creative, and symbolic; try to create parity between students from large colleges and small colleges in terms of their welcome events; ensure that events and activities do not overlap; etc.).
- Consider ways to integrate and align messaging across inventions (e.g., eLearning and required seminars) into a coherent effort. For example, align communications, education, and interventions around alcohol and drugs, diversity and climate, relationship violence and sexual misconduct, wellness, student success. Perhaps run Welcome Week like a conference, with required sessions.
- Create or designate a person, unit, or office to help organize the first-year experience around a common set of goals and outcomes. Have a strategic plan for the first year, which all senior officials and stakeholders agree to implement.

2. *Enhance the campus's capacity to manage student and parent transition through communication and coherence.* There is a lack of strategic messaging with scaffolded support across transitions milestones. This leads to a lack of connectivity among institutional priorities.

3. *Promote data collection and sharing and use across units.* There are overlapping mandates, competition, and lack of transparency at senior levels of leadership. This creates conflicting priorities and agendas around student transitions.

For the most part, this project dwells in the cocurriculum, in advising, and in a set of business operations that have experience implications. The most significant challenge in the project has been that those professionals involved in transitions work don't necessarily see themselves as engaged in supporting student transitions. They are advisors, admissions officers, or faculty. They advise, admit, or teach. A good analogy is that many professionals who write for a living (think of lawyers) don't think of themselves as "writers" or even as people who spend much of their time writing. Identity, role, and activities are a complicated mix. Furthermore, our colleagues are, quite understandably, focused on their own programs and efforts, believe that theirs are strong programs, and worry, again quite reasonably, that they will lose autonomy and agency if, for example, new student orientation needs to coordinate more seamlessly with courses in the first-year curriculum.

Given these complications, the work to date has yielded a set of recommendations tailored to create experiences that help students develop a sense of belonging, and, we hope, identify with the university. The first recommendation was to create a set of goals and outcomes associated with the first-year transition, map the outcomes to interventions, and ensure consistency and continuity of messaging. This is a simple backward design recommendation that also enables messaging to students before they come to MSU, during programs like orientation and at key moments during the first year. As most persons involved with programs that fall under a transitions umbrella understand, messaging is a key value and sometimes a real problem. The design process produced a recommendation to limit the volume of information delivered prior to arrival on campus and extend the welcome period and orientation activities into the fall semester. This approach to transitions also intends to change time in relation to these learning activities. The team also plans to extend orientation and transitions activity into the spring semester.

The design process also identified significant gaps in how programming met the needs of students, particularly those students for whom transition-related programming is most needed, such as first-generation students for whom attending university is novel. The team recommended enhancing the quality and impact of existing welcome events, as well as the equity of these events for diverse students, such as making our welcome convocation more meaningful, creative, and symbolic and trying to create parity between students from large and small colleges. New student orientation has changed the language used to name programs and how programs are designed to align with explicit diversity, equity, and inclusion needs and expectations.

What we have named *transitions* is a space and set of experiences that would not typically be included in a learning design portfolio, but the experiences nested here are clearly learning experiences and arguably some of the most critical experiences for student wellness, well-being, and retention. Indeed, as the *Horizon Report* notes, "the impacts of the refreshed learning design field go beyond online learning or on-campus courses. LDs are becoming involved in areas such as co-curricular projects, experiential learning initiatives, and programs for first-generation students."[23] One of the key design interventions in this effort was to understand this as one experience and not as a set of discrete programs. Another related intervention was to apply service design principles and practices to the process, a move that was experienced as unusual, but not necessarily unwelcome, by participants, and did yield new insights. But if we can get this design project right— and get the people right as part of the process—then any university will be substantially different and almost certainly more effective.

A Discipline or a Profession

To close, we take up a key thread in Kim and Maloney's book on learning innovation, and that is how best to sustain the practice of learning innovation in higher education. They note that while there are a number of professional organizations devoted to learning innovation and an ecosystem for sharing, there are no "associations/conferences devoted to studying these activities."[24] This means that we have little capacity to understand or sustain this activity in higher education. They argue for "chart[ing] a course that adopts some of the elements and expectations of an interdisciplinary academic field. We hope to retain those attributes that have made those practicing learning innovation dynamic and inclusive while also locating its work within the framework of accepted scholarship and criticism."[25]

As the authors of the *Horizon Report* also argue, "learning designers, more than ever before, are being seen as leading experts in teaching and learning on their campuses. They are shifting from service/ support roles to being seen as essential collaborators on the design of learning experiences."[26] Essential to their leadership role on campus is an applied understanding of organizational structures and processes. Ranging from leadership and institutional governance to adaptation processes and strategic change management, learning experience designers will need to complement their (inter)disciplinary knowledge with principles of organizational studies in higher education.[27] More importantly, they will need to be adept at understanding and navigating the power relationships among academics, administrators, and leaders in which their projects are embedded.

The argument that Kim and Maloney make for moving toward an (inter)discipline is fundamentally political, in the sense that the ability to "ask difficult questions, take risks, and challenge institutional assumptions" requires status and agency.[28] A more academic, disciplinary orientation toward learning design and innovation conceivably affords the protections of academic freedom, which includes protections for critique. We are sympathetic to this line of reasoning and wish to build on it. Our sympathy is a function of a few related issues, including our own institutional experience with the Hub and the willingness of disciplinary faculty to recognize the work and the people as valuable.[29]

However, we are not at all sure that doubling down on traditional institutional patterns and habits is a way forward. For instance, the formation of fields, let alone new disciplines, is an exceptionally long process, one measured in lifetimes. One of us (Jeff), has spent his entire career in the emergent field/discipline of Rhetoric and Composition. This is a field that traces its lineage back to antiquity and can trace a long history through higher education since the Middle Ages. But its contemporary existence in the United States is a function of two issues: the emergence of an interest in writing instruction corresponding with the rise of open admissions in the 1970s (the first PhD programs in Rhetoric and Composition started in 1980), and the massive growth in communication studies after the 1950s, which slowly (and then quickly) pushed out rhetoric (speech) in favor of new cognitive studies of communication. Rhetoric and Composition therefore exists now largely in English departments, increasingly in newly created departments, and sometimes dispersed across communication studies and schools of information. Most faculty in this new field or discipline can't yet agree on names, locations, shared commitments, and modes of making knowledge. It will take another lifetime to settle those issues. This is no way to make a disciplinary living.

Then, of course, there is the issue of how the work of innovation in higher education lines up with the values and work practices of disciplinary research faculty. It has not been our experience that tenured or tenure track faculty have much interest in the core learning work of the institution. Indeed, some of the most spectacular failures in our "failure file" have been the result of faculty pulling back from commitments to learning innovation once they realize how much time and energy it takes. The opportunity cost is always research. As faculty note in these situations, research intensive universities don't value faculty spending time on teaching and learning. This is sometimes truer at universities striving to be ranked as more research-intensive. Fields, disciplines, and the departmental structures that manage them are conservative. This can be a feature of university life, but with regard to our work, it is a bug.

Kim and Maloney acknowledge the pushback they've received to their argument for a new (inter)discipline: that it already exists (largely in the fields and disciplines collected in a college of education), that their thinking is an unwelcome intrusion in the space of centers for teaching and learning, and the issue we have raised here—that their idea simply reproduces values and ways of working that are antithetical to changing higher education.[30] A new (inter)discipline may be required, but it may also be true that universities, if they are truly going to change, need to rethink more fundamentally how they are organized and staffed. Indeed, we think the greatest threat to learning design and innovation isn't its lack of disciplinarity but rather that it isn't professionalized and institutionalized in a way that enables careers.

Career trajectories matter. Consider the remarkably truncated structure of academic career trajectories in higher education. If we look at the business side of colleges and universities, there are highly professionalized roles with clear structures for career advancement in information technology, housing, operations, and in some cases, student services. Professionals in these roles can have careers at a given institution, but they can also have careers across the sector. They have professional associations and recognized expertise. On the academic side of the institution, we have the tenure system and then a patchwork of names, roles, and quasi-systems with varying levels of contingency and value. Even in the tenure system, the roles are cookie-cutter (or experienced in that way): 40 percent of your time on this, 40 percent on that, and 20 percent over there. These are intellectually expansive lives (often) with high levels of autonomy (notionally), but with extraordinarily little flexibility. But there is a career path. One can be promoted. Twice. Yet this is more than what is possible for academic professionals outside of that system.

An alternative (or complement) to disciplinarity is institutional change. This alternative isn't much easier, but it is likely necessary for innovation work to persist as a feature of institutional life in higher education. As Kim and Maloney note, organizations like the Hub exist now largely because of a "magical provost" who creates new opportunities for innovation that don't last beyond his or her tenure (this may be truer for us than makes us comfortable). The required institutional adaptation, however, may not be to make a discipline but rather to make this space a highly professionalized feature of how the organization thinks.

To understand the university as an experience, to intentionally design that experience, and to take human experiences seriously as a subject requiring deep inquiry is a radical idea. Most universities have all the tools necessary to prioritize experience design and learning innovation. What might not be the case is the extent to which these "tools" are purposed appropriately. LXD is our focus here, of course, because it is the keystone activity and profession for our larger argument. With that, we think it is important to close this section by returning to purpose and passion—to the need to design as if we give a damn.[31] To suggest that our purpose must be grounded in something like giving a damn might seem obvious (of course we do!) or offensive to suggest (how dare you!). Yet universities are large and complex institutions and are not immune to common human and organizational dynamics. As Madsbjerg reminds us:

> A lack of care is often at the root of many of the business and organizational challenges I encounter in my consulting. Over time, as management has become increasingly professionalized, you can sense a kind of nihilism or loss of meaning in the executive layers. This nihilism is strongest in large corporate cultures where management is seen as a profession in and of itself, with no strong connection to what the company actually makes or does. What happens when satisfaction in work comes from managing—reorganizing, optimizing the operation, hiring new people, and making strategies—and not from producing something meaningful?[32]

What happens, in Madsbjerg's experience, is that products and services fail and employees drift and lose passion for their work. Universities are not immune. It is easy for educators of all kinds, and for those who lead and manage them, to get captured by routines, assume a shared purpose, and therefore lose track of why universities exist. It is also easy to think about learning experience design only in terms of courses and technologies. It is easy to lose track of our value because it is easy to think that we are in the idea creation and delivery business and not in the experience business. We can, therefore, forget about people and how they experience our universities.

People—students, families, community partners, staff, and faculty—are key to our existence and success. Indeed, it puts the totality of what it means to experience Michigan State University (in our case) on the table, and it puts human beings, particularly those most vulnerable or at risk, at the center of our work. To focus on the *experience* changes everything about what it means to design for higher education, from the class, to the program, to the culture—and everything in between. This is why higher education needs LXD and needs the expertise of learning experience designers to lead these changes. In chapter 2, we describe how to operationalize LXD to translate aspirational changes into practical, actionable steps.

2

Operationalizing Design

IN CHAPTER 1, we argued for the primacy of *experience* in learning experience design (LXD) and the cognitive, social, and affective opportunities possible from such a focus. This chapter builds on that effort and sits as the second of a three-chapter sequence that articulates our theory and practice of design in higher education. Here we focus on operationalizing our own design practice through a set of principles that extends the conceptual descriptions of LXD into our own specific design process. In chapter 3, we will focus on conversation design, which is the label we give to the discursive space we create for others to solve problems and realize opportunities.

Our operationalization of LXD is based on the following principles:

- LXD focuses on learning and must do so by drawing from the learning sciences to conceptualize how people learn and how humans function in different learning environments. We want learning experiences to be equitable and transformative for students.
- LXD focuses on the human experience and must do so by way of thoughtful applications of human-centered design processes to

understand what inspires students, faculty, and stakeholders. We want to offer learning experiences that people can connect with and that create new opportunities for them.

- LXD also focuses on design knowledge from theory and from industries that focus on experience design. We want learning experiences to be simultaneously practical and engaging, like the best services we experience in our lives.

These principles might seem obvious given the phrase "learning experience design," but we believe they are far from obvious when we get into the weeds of a design process. In our own practice, we commonly confront questions about how to apply learning experience design to help create better versions of higher education and how to use designerly ways of thinking to achieve the institution's learning experience goals. We constantly wrestle with how to gain a better understanding of what works and what doesn't work in specific learning experiences.

Our approach to design combines key foundations in design thinking, systems thinking, and futures thinking. These ways of thinking are the roots of our educational design practice, and we remix these ideas in ways suited to address the challenges of our own higher education context and organizational culture. This constant remixing of methods has gotten us to the point where we have a stable, yet flexible, approach tuned to the needs of higher education change projects. The challenges our partners wish to address may start in the domain of learning, but they often necessitate understanding the systems required to successfully implement creative, future-oriented learning solutions. We need ways of thinking embedded in flexible processes that will help our colleagues grow in their design inquiries. In some ways, the context of higher education is analogous to that of other industries. In other ways, higher education is a quite different context. We've built our approach by doing the work, practicing these approaches, and continuing to iterate as we go. In this chapter, we discuss the roots of our design practice and discuss how we have operationalized our practice through our design process and patterns.

Design Thinking, Systems Thinking, and Futures Thinking

Milev argues that design has always been fundamental to our survival as symbol makers. While we most often think of design as a specialized field, it is useful to remember that it is an ancient human ability.[1] It is fundamental. Looking at the technologies in our pockets, the dashboard of our cars, and the shape of our lived experiences, it is easy, as Clark and Brody so aptly summarize, to understand that "design is everywhere" because the "modern world is artificial, it is a world that we have made and designed and keep on remaking and redesigning."[2] The ability to assess a current moment, conceive of a better one, and then make it exist, is one of the things that makes us human, enables our imaginations, and gives us agency in our lives. Design is fundamentally about making and changing the world around us.

It is true that this human practice has given rise to highly specialized design fields that take as their focus the design of products, services, and even whole organizations. These more specialized processes of design are often focused on what Rittel and Webber have described as "wicked problems," those complex issues that have multiple and competing causes and potential solutions and that place the designers in a position where the ground underneath them is constantly shifting.[3] It's clear that design practices adapted for higher education are sorely needed. Most people in higher education have simply never seen or experienced design as applied to their own work or their organizational life. The infrastructure and processes of higher education are siloed, slow, and hierarchical, which produces highly structured, top-down ways of making decisions that focus on the expertise of those present "in the room." If you are allowed in the room, you get to make the decisions. Even then, decisions are made based on power, status, influence, and access to resources within the social structure of those in the room.[4] There is no design there.

Therefore, we have had to develop a design process to move people, from a lack of understanding of design and a built-in reticence to behave differently, to a place in which they are willing to prototype elements of a new process, practice, or organizational structure they're attempting to make. To get there, we have chosen and remixed elements of design thinking into a design process that we believe to be useful for higher education.

Design thinking has been described in many ways: a process for problem-solving, a mindset, an attitude at the core of a designer's practice, but also sometimes an "innovation theater."[5] Given the considerable attention design thinking has attracted, the idea has grown to combine approaches from multiple fields outside of design, such as business. We are particularly fond of understanding design thinking to involve "empathy for alternate contexts, framing of problems and opportunities, ideation of multiple solutions, validation of executions."[6] Its titular origins can be traced to Rowe's *Design Thinking*.[7] Its methods in our popular imagination are often traced to both the design consultancy IDEO and Stanford's d.School. Its fundamental intellectual origins can perhaps best be traced to the 1960s and *The Conference on Systematic and Intuitive Methods in Engineering, Industrial Design, Architecture and Communication*, where scholars such as Herbert Simon, Horst Rittel, Melvin Webber, and Victor Papanek argued for where design best fit as a field and just what sorts of problems design was best suited to address.[8] Since this time, design thinking has captured the popular imagination and has been applied across contexts. And it can work. Because of this and because the fundamentals of thinking like a designer privilege creativity and require research, we find thinking in these ways useful. Innovation and change in higher education is, indeed, wicked hard.

Having said this, we have a complicated relationship with *design thinking*. Our initial reception inside Michigan State University associated us with both design thinking and *innovation* (no surprise there.) This language can have negative connotations in higher education because of the association with *disruption* and Silicon Valley. It was easy to dismiss our approach as a passing fad. It is also true that we have seen and experienced vapid applications of design thinking. We also sometimes work with the typical props of the trade: sticky notes, dry erase markers, whiteboards, and even some Play-Doh. In "serious" higher education culture, this can be risky behavior. Yet such tools allow us to create generative spaces through which we can make a different educational reality with project partners. It has allowed us to better understand the core of the experience that our partners are hoping for, map the system they are working in, and prototype and test possible solutions. These techniques are useful. They allow us to practice thinking as a designer with others. Most often, however, our language centers on "design," which is the most common language used in this book. By design we intend to signal a deeper intellectual practice, which encompasses design thinking as it is typically understood. But the mix of ideas that informs our process doesn't end here.

Our remixing requires *systems thinking* as well. Systems thinking has become an essential frame for navigating the layers of change necessary for our design work. Conway, Masters, and Thorold recommend that, in order to solve complex problems, design thinking needs to be accompanied by systems thinking to impact complex systems.[9] That is, "great design doesn't always generate impact" without attempts to scale and create systemic change.[10] Impact requires understanding the context as well as anticipating barriers that can impede design implementation (more on this in chapter 4).

Systems thinking began with the work of Jay Forrester and the Systems Dynamic Group at MIT and is a holistic and dynamic approach to seeing the relationships between separate elements of a system. This approach helps us best understand how one part of the system might influence others: "Systems design methods are able to zoom in and out based on need, moving from macro-views of service ecologies to micro-views of product interfaces."[11] Systems thinking also helps individuals to understand their mental models or schemas, and how these might influence their perspectives and behaviors in the world. Systems thinking has been popularized over the last thirty years by scholars such as Senge and Meadows, who have used it to help private and public organizations better understand their complex, entrenched behaviors.[12] Senge and Meadows take inspiration from the biology of the natural world to point out how to change components in systems to produce hoped-for growth. Senge has certainly inspired our work, as he has provided key conceptual grounding for the building of "learning organizations" that "continually expand their capacity to create the results they truly desire, where new and expansive patterns of thinking are nurtured, where collective aspiration is set free, and where people are continually learning to see the whole together."[13] In short, then, systems thinking has been crucial for understanding the overall context, boundaries, and scope of our projects. It has helped us to frame projects within the "complex reality of the university as an organization possessing its own structures, cultures, and practices."[14]

Design in higher education must be future-facing as well, often courageously so, and both design and systems thinking are rooted in the present (with brief glimpses into the past).[15] When it comes to innovation, futures thinking can help people identify trends and opportunities. It can also help people imagine how to seize new opportunities, because "futuring" in these ways can be usefully disruptive to commonplace ways of thinking. It is possible to unlock the imaginations of even the most recalcitrant faculty to map alternative, challenging, and relevant futures for themselves and their students.[16] As a group creates "memories of the future,"[17] the outcomes can provide guidance across three dimensions: strategic guidance, a shared vision for innovation portfolios, and identifying innovation initiatives by looking at the requirements for the design process. Therefore, we are grounded in a mix of design thinking, systems thinking, and futures thinking. We pull our commitment to *learning experience* through this process, and we use process to create and facilitate productive conversations with and for partners (see chapter 3 for much more on the importance of conversation). All this is easy to say. The point of this chapter, however, is to close the gap between theory and practice. In order to make clear to partners our ways of thinking about design in the service of project execution, we had to come up with a model that could operationalize our ideas and provide repeatable guidance to the larger Hub team. We needed a process that was tuned to the cultures and tolerances of higher education (e.g., a hard push toward divergent thinking to hedge rushes to solutions.) We needed to translate our conceptual understanding of design processes into practice, and to gather around a set of common practices and language. Operationalizing our process meant being able to optimize, measure, and share with others what our work "did." Shields and Rangarajan link operationalization to the measurement of otherwise difficult-to-grasp concepts.[18] For instance, in medicine, the concept of "health" might be operationalized by indicators like weight, exercise, or diet. In the social sciences, an intangible phenomenon that cannot be directly measured, such as anxiety, is often operationalized into elements that are observable. In our case, operationalizing design ideas into process meant creating common language and practice.

Operationalizing Design Theories into Process

Operationalizing any process is hard work, particularly when the goal is to preserve the richness of design and resist reduction to a set of steps or rules. Teal explains that often those with backgrounds in scientific methods or representational thinking are "primed to alter the fluidness of design thinking to fit with the linear causal schemas that they have been brought up on."[19] Academics are superprimed in these ways. The challenge in working with campus partners and stakeholders, then, is to shift to a model and mindset that progresses through a series of iterations to tackle complex issues through creative problem-solving. To do so also makes it possible to work against "solutionism," or the rush to solve problems too quickly. We address this issue more fully later in the book, but in higher education in particular, solutionism is a serious threat. Higher education is full of smart people with considerable expertise and confidence. Get a few of them in a room, and they can quickly and confidently solve most problems, especially for other people. We believe that we should be more iterative, participatory, and modest. Design processes must enable those virtues.

Those familiar with design and design thinking will recognize our clear adoption of the British Design Council's Double Diamond design process, IDEO's human-centered design process, and Stanford d. School's design thinking process (figure 2.1).[20] We used it as a baseline as we developed our own language and practice, because we found this

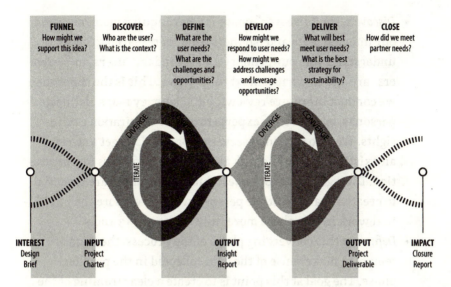

FUNNEL
How might we support this idea?

DISCOVER
Who are the user?
What is the context?

DEFINE
What are the user needs?
What are the challenges and opportunities?

DEVELOP
How might we respond to user needs?
How might we address challenges and leverage opportunities?

DELIVER
What will best meet user needs?
What is the best strategy for sustainability?

CLOSE
How did we meet partner needs?

DIVERGE · CONVERGE · ITERATE · DIVERGE · CONVERGE · ITERATE

INTEREST
Design Brief

INPUT
Project Charter

OUTPUT
Insight Report

OUTPUT
Project Deliverable

IMPACT
Closure Report

Figure 2.1. The Hub Design Process

visual provided easily accessible anchors while being flexible enough for us to adapt in ways that fit higher education. And we did adapt as we learned (and continue to do so). We reshaped the visual elements (curving lines to emphasize movement and ongoing iteration), and we revised the prompting questions in each stage to better fit our context and to emphasize the systems thinking and futures thinking elements of our work. This visual, in other words, isn't eye candy. It is an operationalization of framing questions and required deliverables.

The following moments shape our process:

- *Funnel:* At this point in the design process, we ask questions of fit and focus for potential design work. As project partners from across campus bring potential challenges, opportunities, and intended outcomes for the (re)design of university programs, we ask, How might we support this idea? To decide how to best support a partner's idea, we put together a design brief and a project charter that outline the planning and organizational processes that result either in the creation of a project or in us directing a potential project partner to other collaborators on campus.

- *Discover:* The "discover" phase is a key inquiry moment, when our internal team and partners conduct research to better understand who our primary and secondary "users" or "learners" are and in what context they evolve. This is the time when we conduct literature reviews, build journey maps, delineate personas, or interview experts to gather inspiration and insights. We also rely on observation protocols to get a sense of an existing setting and look at analogous examples for inspiration. Divergence and openness during this phase are essential to creativity and multiple perspectives. We explore the intellectual work in this phase more fully in chapters 3 and 5.
- *Define:* In this converging phase of the process, the team attempts to make sense of the data collected in the previous phase. The goal at this point is to create a clear framing of the challenge through guiding insights. Brainstorming sessions help organize and make sense of the data. The data is grouped and structured to identify what areas of needs or interest will be pursued in the project; these are then synthesized into findings. At the end of this phase of the project, an insight report is created to ensure that all collaborators are on the same page.
- *Develop:* The start of the second diamond phase represents the beginning of divergent development. This is when solutions start to be shaped, prototyped, and tested. Workshops, mapping sessions, and collaborative design critiques are the hallmarks of this phase of the design process. Oftentimes, we brief and then charter a new phase of a project because the work and sometimes the people have changed. The design brief is used once again to propel the project. Feedback is collected from the different prototypes and incorporated into the implementation of a solution. This data is used to inform the team, partners, and stakeholders in order to finalize a proposed solution.
- *Deliver:* In this phase, the designed solution is launched to address the needs identified in the initial phases. Testing, iterations, and revisions guide this convergent phase as the solution

is shared with a broader audience for feedback. The outcome of this phase is the project deliverable that was outlined in the project charter. Through iterations of assessment and approval, the solution is launched or released to collaborators on campus for further iterations. As this concludes our involvement with partners and the scope of our initial work, this is when the charter is either closed or reevaluated for future steps. We are committed to execution, and so "shipping product" is a core value. Too often in higher education, ideation is strong, and execution is weak. Too often we fail to close loops on pilots and prototypes, which prevent us from learning. Failure to deliver will cause design work in higher education to fail.

- *Close:* Closing a project, much like the funnel phase, involves asking questions of focus to partners. As we write a closure report, we not only outline what our deliverables were but also reflect on the process itself as well as on our role guiding partners through a design experience to support their creation of transformative and equitable learning experiences. It is important to note that closing a project does not end a collaboration, but instead functions as a new steppingstone for future partnerships.

There are several virtues to a shared representation of a design process, developed as it has been over a period of time and via a fair number of failures and successes. The common language and practices create transparency and ensure that the entire team is focused on people, their experiences, and on execution. Transparency, particularly given that higher education cultures can lack transparency, is fundamental. By making thinking visible through process and project documentation created to identify ongoing questions, doubts, or reflections, we contribute to both our own understanding as well as the partner's understanding of the design process as it unfolds.[21] Each phase of our process is focused on human experience in the form of our default *user* questions (we shift from *user* to other, often more appropriate terms, depending on the context of the project). As we argue in chapter 1, learning experience design must focus on humanizing problem-solving and creative processes, on understanding human experiences (getting people right), and on carefully building relationships to ensure that collaboration with partners and stakeholders on campus is effective. The rich literature on behavioral change tells us that for a change intention (we want to redesign our program) to be implemented (we are redesigning our program), all sorts of people issues need to be considered. A design process such as ours doesn't guarantee outcomes, but the process lives our values. Our practice lives in relationships, which means accounting for how best to align attitudes, subjective norms, and perceived behavioral control.[22]

We insist on execution, which is the way we hold ourselves accountable. Our projects deliver, and this is one way we build and maintain relationships. Our moments of delivery are also intentional moments of reflection. For that purpose, we have embedded documented reflective moments in our processes through design briefs, project charters, insight reports, and closure reports. As we move through the different phases of a project, it is therefore important for us to document our observations about partners' reactions, comments, or fears that emerge, because they inform our systemic view of the design process. Designers tend to have the ability to solve problems intuitively. Yet, identifying what drives design intuition in our practices is challenging for that very reason. Design decisions ought to be linked to evidence or data that supports our process with partners. The goal of design thinking is indeed to make thinking visible.[23] Wendt sees "writing as an intermediary between decontextualized, armchair-style thinking and full prototyping. It allows a designer to consciously articulate intentions, scenarios, and possible outcomes by crafting a story in which one can easily see missing pieces or conflicting messages."[24] These reflective exercises help us think about how best to support a team in implementing a behavior in question.[25]

Being transparent in our work certainly exposes moments of vulnerability for all participants.[26] Vulnerable moments allow for creativity, innovation, and change, and perhaps most importantly, they also help us tell the story of our work. Indeed, the very first drafts of this book can be found in our project documentation and reflection. As Brené Brown famously said in her TedTalk on the power of vulnerability, "maybe stories are just data with a soul."[27] The reason why our reporting and reflective exercises are important in making thinking (and data) visible is because they help us identify storytelling moments. Stories are ways for us to communicate with partners and stakeholders, but also to share with diverse audiences the impact of their (re)designs on teaching and learning. Indeed, "we mostly rely on stories to put out ideas into context and give them meaning."[28] Tim Brown, CEO of IDEO, explains that "it is essential that storytelling begin early in the life of a project and be woven into every aspect of the innovation effort. It has been common practice for design teams to bring writers in . . . to document a project once it has been completed. Increasingly they are building them into the design team from day one to help move the story along in real time."[29] In this spirit, the next section continues the story of our design process by moving through a case project and a set of related examples to let project details bring the process to life. In doing so, we move from model to messy.

Learning Experience Design in Practice

The design process has been successful in helping us work, but we want to emphasize that it is not one size fits all. We make adaptations as we go. This should be obvious, but we find most discussions of design practice to be too clean, too cookie-cutter, and we don't want our own version of a double diamond to be seen as a static representation of an idealized way of working. Although the representation of our process seems to be linear, the process itself is not. Different phases intersect and interact with one another in circular ways, creating pathways between stages that influence the project. This is easier to demonstrate via some examples.

The primary case in this chapter is the story of the iOS Design Lab. The lab was launched as an experience that prepares learners for innovation in a digital economy. By bringing design, coding, and entrepreneurship together within Apple's iOS ecosystem, the lab was created as a space to amplify learners' existing skills with the integrative mindset needed in our global economy and society. The iOS Design Lab stands for the following:

- *"iOS" is the tool:* We help learners understand the importance of computing skills and practice the basics of coding in Apple's language, Swift. We follow *Apple's Everyone Can Code* curriculum and use a variety of activities—sometimes without technology—to familiarize learners with ways to solve problems with technology.
- *"Design" is the method:* We use a challenge-based learning (CBL) approach to encourage learners to address challenges in their communities through research, planning, and engagement with users. Design is both a verb and a noun in this process. Learners design their way through prototyping their ideas based on a solid foundation.
- *"Lab" is the mindset:* We aim to create a learning space similar to a lab, where learners can try and fail safely, and where they work in teams to brainstorm and creatively solve problems. It is a space where they learn to communicate, set expectations for their team, and collaborate with people from different backgrounds and value other perspectives on their work.

The following phases guided our process:

Funnel: The Hub entered discussions with Apple as an intellectual partner to craft a design brief about the potential for creating a new learning opportunity for undergraduate students that would introduce them to coding in Swift, Apple's programming language, while teaching them about app design and development within the iOS ecosystem. We asked how we might support this new learning experience. After a set of conversations and the identification of campus partners, the project charter was written to outline roles and responsibilities, as well as potential objectives and key results to anticipate for the project.

Discover: This divergent phase was guided by the questions: Who are the students who would be interested in this learning experience? What drives them? Why would they join? What could this experience bring to their academic, professional, or personal journey? We gathered information from a variety of sources for this inquiry phase: student focus groups, landscape analyses on existing offerings at other universities, and research literatures on computing, design, and entrepreneurship education. We also looked at Apple's challenge-based learning model as a curricular example. We conducted this inquiry using futures thinking tools—that is, we aimed to gather strategic foresight to create an experience that would benefit students in the present as well as in the future. The app economy is constantly evolving, and one insight of the discovery phase in this project was that we needed to embed coding, design, and entrepreneurship knowledge within a framework of critical skills that would persist through time in the app economy: creative problem-solving, teamwork and collaboration, and strategic communication.

Define: The team started converging in the "define" phase by gathering all the data we had collected. We clustered the information into themes and categories and sorted them to produce an insight report. The insight report shaped our in-depth intuitive understanding of the opportunity space. We continued conducting student focus groups during that phase to receive feedback and ensure that our insights resonated with different student populations. We asked students to help us frame the learning experience by giving them agency in participatory design sessions. For instance, students decided on the name "iOS Design Lab" as a reflection of the tool, the method, and the mindset they wanted to explore in the experience. We also included campus partners and stakeholders in the conversations to ensure that the design was evaluated from different disciplinary perspectives, pedagogical viewpoints, and administrative lenses. The insight report constituted the basis for the next design phase, in which we started developing the curriculum itself.

Develop: Once the team gathered enough information to create a prototype of the learning experience, we mapped out the curriculum and associated activities as the starting point of the second diamond in our design process. We worked backward from a set of outcomes we wanted to see in the experience. We wanted students to

1. learn the basics of Swift;
2. understand the relevance of app design in the development process;
3. frame their work with an entrepreneurial mindset; and
4. engage in collaborative participation with others.

This phase was characterized by divergent development among the instructional team—ideas started to be shaped, prototyped, and tested. We conducted a series of curricular mapping sessions to explore opportunities and best options to design the learning experience. We requested and incorporated feedback from students, colleagues, and partners on the different versions of the curricular prototypes we had designed, and we presented our progress to our team and stakeholders to finalize a proposed curriculum for the iOS Design Lab before piloting the experience itself.

Deliver—Iteration 1: The first iteration of the lab helped us refine the curriculum, receive feedback from students and partners, and gather data for future prototypes of the experience, including space, content, pace, teamwork, and recruitment. Students in the first iteration knew they were piloting the iOS Design Lab with us and were considered co-designers of the experience. This helped the instructional team better understand student needs, further elaborate relationships with Apple, and continue envisioning what elements needed to be integrated into its design. For instance, although the first iteration was supposed to last one semester, the instructional team and the students realized that there was more to cover than the time allotted. This resulted in expanding the experience to the entire academic year. Students also indicated that they wanted to gain more experience with app design. We therefore added more design-related activities in the curriculum.

One difficulty the instructional team faced was assigning challenges for students to solve through app design: too prescriptive and it dampened their motivation and creativity; too vague and it discouraged them. We also quickly realized that access to devices was an issue. We were relying on students to use their own laptops, but we knew this would eventually become a limitation. Finally, while we used the *Apple Everyone Can Code* curriculum for Swift, we observed that students learned better by exploring code in their own groups. We took all these findings gathered through observations and conversations with students into our second iteration of the experience.

Deliver—Iteration 2: A second year was launched based on the feedback and observations gathered in the first iteration. To ensure continuity, two students from the first cohort joined the instructional team in the second iteration. The student coaches helped with the instructional team and also guided students in the experience, shared advice, discussed their experiences, and encouraged others. In that iteration, we purchased devices for the group to make sure that everyone had access to the same tools. We also expanded contact time during the week and designed a set of challenges that were framed around campus issues to give students a scope of work they could solve through app development. We added our campus entrepreneurship librarian to the instructional team to help students further understand the importance of research in app development—an issue we had faced in the first iteration, with teams jumping to solutions without conducting proper research.

The new emphasis on research brought both challenges and opportunities. On the one hand, teams made better-informed choices related to their designs. They learned where to search for relevant data and to make data-driven decisions for the direction their apps were taking. On the other hand, the emphasis on research slowed the process considerably, and even with more contact hours, the instructional team found it difficult to move to design and coding without rushing students through a necessary inquiry phase. This second iteration concluded with the COVID-19 pandemic, and we had to shut down campus before the students' final app showcase.

Close: Our engagement with that project ended after two iterations of development. After completing our deliverable and closing our char-

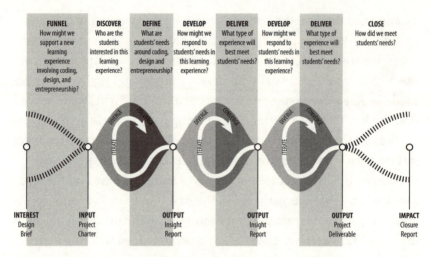

FUNNEL	DISCOVER	DEFINE	DEVELOP	DELIVER	DEVELOP	DELIVER	CLOSE
How might we support a new learning experience involving coding, design, and entrepreneurship?	Who are the students interested in this learning experience?	What are students' needs around coding, design and entrepreneurship?	How might we respond to students' needs in this learning experience?	What type of experience will best meet students' needs?	How might we respond to students' needs in this learning experience?	What type of experience will best meet students' needs?	How did we meet students' needs?

INTEREST	INPUT		OUTPUT	OUTPUT	OUTPUT		IMPACT
Design Brief	Project Charter		Insight Report	Insight Report	Project Deliverable		Closure Report

Figure 2.2. The iOS Design Lab Design Process

ter, the iOS Design Lab was ready to move from its incubation phase at the Hub for Innovation in Learning and Technology to a more stable collaborative relationship between our College of Arts and Letters and our College of Business. The Hub design process not only guided the team through the four different phases of design but also allowed us, through that process, to build lasting relationships on campus and beyond to establish the sustainability of that experience.

We started the project with the intention to prototype a learning experience that responded to needs in the workplace and on our campus—a need for experiential learning offerings around coding and design, a way to address the lack of diversity and representation in computing, and an opportunity for students to better understand and participate in the app economy. In addition, that space afforded us the opportunity to engage in an intellectual collaboration with Apple as a partner. The design process for this learning experience is illustrated in figure 2.2.

The iOS Design Lab project has progressed through three iterations to date. The key feature of the project has been high-fidelity prototyping. This enabled us to start fast, with the understanding that we would iterate over time. The design process led the iOS Design Lab team

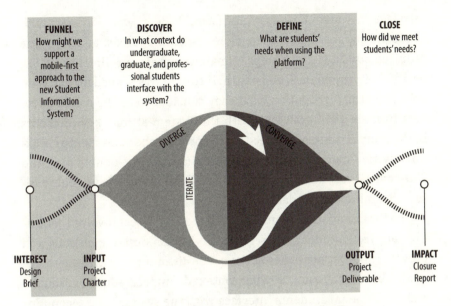

Figure 2.3. The Student Information System Design Process

to work with students to codesign a learning experience that fostered teamwork, interdisciplinary collaborations, and creative problem-solving. This project followed the Hub design process quite closely, and we credit the process with providing a necessary framework for us. Each of our projects follows its own trajectory, and the double-diamond process is stretched in different directions in order to fulfill specific project outcomes. In the case of the iOS Design Lab, the nature of the project enabled a specific expression of our process. We owned this project, which meant we could start quickly and had strong buy-in from participants. We designed with students and faculty involved in the Lab experiences themselves, heightening both transparency and accountability. And we focused on prototyping. This gave us frequent moments for insight reporting, reflection, and storytelling. This project has proven to be a rich context for design.

Another and quite different process is visible in the work we did on the university's implementation of a new student information system (SIS) (figure 2.3). We focused on a new set of adaptive web interfaces for the system and created initial design direction for a native mobile interface. Through these user interfaces, students would interact with academic support units, their own academic records, and complete required administrative steps to maintain their enrollment at MSU, verify their attendance, and pay their tuition. We argued for and then collected student input on what they consider to be the most important functional interactions with the system at four key moments in the year. Because of the needs of the project, the team spent approximately two months in the first two phases of the double diamond ("discover" and "define"), focusing solely on inquiry work, doing research, and collecting data.

The first set of inquiry questions in the SIS project involved collecting data from student focus groups to inform design questions and provide input for possible solutions. The *discover* phase was therefore guided by the question, In what context do undergraduate, graduate, and professional students interface with the system? The second inquiry question in the *define* phase—What are students' needs when using the platform?—was meant to gather student feedback on possible prototypes and validate design solution ideas. Because the scope of the Hub's involvement in this project resulted in a recommendation report as its deliverable, only the first part of the double diamond is represented here. In complex, large-scale projects on campus, we may scope short-term engagements with partners to provide them with key information or data from direct user experience. In these cases, we focus mostly on the inquiry phase in order to jump-start a development phase that might not include us.

More recently, the Hub collaborated with campus partners to proactively design high quality online learning experiences during the COVID-19 epidemic, focusing particularly on student needs, retention, social presence, community building, and connectivity among students and faculty. In the spring and summer of 2020, the Hub and campus partners designed and delivered the necessary professional development (PD) experience for faculty moving their face-to-face courses online, and we prioritized building social presence, connectivity, and an online community. Because of the urgency of the situa-

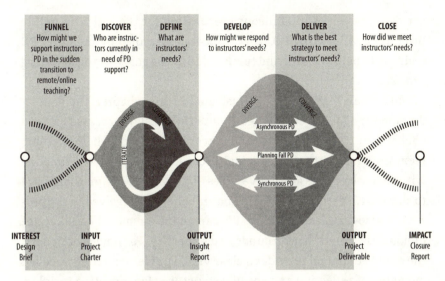

FUNNEL	DISCOVER	DEFINE	DEVELOP	DELIVER	CLOSE
How might we support instructors PD in the sudden transition to remote/online teaching?	Who are instructors currently in need of PD support?	What are instructors' needs?	How might we respond to instructors' needs?	What is the best strategy to meet instructors' needs?	How did we meet instructors' needs?

Asynchronous PD

Planning Fall PD

Synchronous PD

INTEREST	INPUT		OUTPUT		OUTPUT	IMPACT
Design Brief	Project Charter		Insight Report		Project Deliverable	Closure Report

Figure 2.4. The Online Professional Development Design Process

tion, the Hub team spent most of its time in the develop and deliver phases of the double diamond.

The representation in figure 2.4 is quite different from the others presented in this chapter. This project was not only highly collaborative but also required a team drawn from across campus to react quickly to the transition to remote teaching and learning. While there was a bit of inquiry involved through the first diamond (faculty survey, previous PD content, gathering of existing resources), the bulk of the work was pushed to the second diamond, due to the urgency of the situation and the expressed needs of educators on campus. Within the second diamond, three simultaneous iterations were occurring, visible in the three concurrent arrows in the diamond. One was the development and reiteration of an asynchronous professional development (PD) training that responded to immediate teaching needs. The second was the offering of a synchronous PD piloted twice in April and reiterated throughout the summer, with multiple sessions offered to educators. Throughout the summer sessions, changes were made to the training workshop as well as to its facilitation process. The third arrow represents simultaneous preparation for the Fall 2020 online teaching and learning PD. This work was informed by the other PD training to help discover and further define the goals for the following semester.

In the different examples illustrated in this chapter, the double-diamond model as represented in our Hub design process is a good anchor for common language and processes. The model helps the Hub team understand the process and proceed on a delineated timeline with clear objectives and deliverables. It provides a common language to share with external partners and stakeholders involved in the process. It also enables flexibility. We can adapt the model based on individual designers' backgrounds and expertise. For novice designers, the double diamond provides a clear visual guideline with embedded moments of reflection and specific structures for reporting insights. For more experienced designers, the double diamond enables creativity in processes and design practices while following the same structure and process. Learning experience designers can find their niche in specific phases of the process and rely on their expertise to bring that knowledge to the project, whether it is research, prototyping, or development, for instance. But more importantly, the double diamond is meant to be aspirational as we develop projects. It should enable our imaginations and help us structure the unexpected.

Structuring the Unexpected

This is a chapter about our design process, and it fits within a three-chapter sequence intended to build on our understanding of learning experience design (chapter 1) and lead into a more in-depth discussion of the spaces of interaction we design (chapter 3). We have been keen not only to describe our process for others to explore but also to do so with enough detail about how we practice design to expose variation and a bit of messiness. Idealized forms make us nervous, and we hope to have avoided them. As we write in chapter 3, we design conversations that we hope then produce outcomes such as curricula or programs. These conversations are patterns for others to use to solve problems and realize opportunities. We believe in the power of conversations (1) to focus on language as a way to construct reality, (2) to render experiences visible and available as a resource for thinking, (3) to structure how we might talk and listen, and (4) to ground teams in acts of making. What we have provided in this chapter is the structure for that process.

To be sure, most of the problems we address in our work are complex, and we hope some process allows us to manage that complexity. It doesn't matter if the issue is the design or redesign of an existing educational program or holding space for a team to consider how they might work differently together; the work has layers that aren't easily served by a linear, one-size-fits-all approach. The work also isn't well served by having no process or by recourse to thin or empty notions of "design thinking." What is required is a design process that operationalizes a theory of design that can unearth the unexpected, can listen deeply to the needs of project partners, can help us co-create and test potential solutions, and then can assist with the iterative implementation of these solutions. That process "holds" the necessary interactions between stakeholders. We call those interactions "conversations," and we turn our attention to them next.

3

Designing Conversations

IN CHAPTER 2, we outlined what it means to operationalize learning experience design. But when asked for a simple answer about what we do, our answer is "we design conversations." This means we design spaces for others to solve problems and realize opportunities. We value conversations as a way to "unfreeze" problems, identify potential solutions, and prototype ideas with high impact for transformative and equitable learning experiences.[1] The way we support conversations about LXD is necessary to enable innovation in a way that's particularly well attuned to teaching and learning in higher education. This chapter is concerned with describing more fully what we mean by "conversation" and how conversation design can serve as a tool for change.

Higher education is a highly discursive space in which "argument" is the fundamental pattern of engagement. A discussion of conversations would of course be incomplete without acknowledging the research and scholarship on power and organizational theory in higher education.[2] In inhabiting a dialogical space, learning experience designers who conceive of and facilitate conversations have to be knowledgeable, yet critical, about the material, structural, discursive, and affective impacts of power dynamics, exclusion, and inclusion occurring in these conversations.[3] Morley describes how "the higher education sector not only reflects and reinforces social stratification, but, via its production and circulation of narratives and quotidian micropolitical practices, it does difference. It goes without saying that power relations infuse organizational and disciplinary cultures, epistemic and pedagogic traditions, student access, achievement and employability, research priorities, the elitist prestige economy, funding and employment regimes, opportunity structures, academic identities, mobilities and subjectivities."[4] As such, we have been paying a lot of attention to the research on "talk as situated practice"—on how microinteractional behaviors enact power—in order to design conversations for change in teaching and learning in higher education.[5]

Effective conversations are therefore culturally normative as well as essential for moving institutions. Not surprisingly, one of our biggest hurdles has been to get people to talk to each other (and not *at* or *past* each other) about issues of concern for student success on campus. This phenomenon is further amplified by the well-known "functional silo syndrome."[6] Disciplines, which often work as silos, allow for in-depth expertise and advancements in a specific area of knowledge. However, in a time of globalized changes, rapid technological progress, and worldwide disruptions like the COVID-19 pandemic, a siloed structure often leads to missed opportunities for collaboration. While an issue for disciplinary boundaries, it is also true that organizational units (admissions, student affairs, career services, advancement) can also stand in the way of necessary change. We believe that conversations are essential to design because the metaphor and practice of conversations allow us to make thinking visible and to build awareness about the contexts in which change is being infused. Designed conversations slow down institutionalized routines, break down silos, and create momentum around our thoughts, attitudes, intentions, and resistance to change. Bohm and his coauthors argue that through conversation

we become aware that we live in a world produced almost entirely by human enterprise and thus, by human thought. The room in which we sit, the language in which these words are written, our national boundaries, our systems of value, and even that which we take to be our direct perceptions of reality are essentially manifestations of the way human beings think and have thought. We realize that without a willingness to explore this situation and to gain a deep insight into it, the real crises of our time cannot be confronted, nor can we find anything more than temporary solutions to the vast array of human problems that now confront us.[7]

Because of their social nature, conversations require thoughtful consideration of how we create opportunities for discussions that are ethical (transparent about goals and values), collaborative (engaging all participants), innovative (creating new frames of possibilities), and responsible (being answerable for our own actions).[8] Our view of conversations is anchored in a constructivist approach to communication, and we consider shared experiences to be the best way to acquire knowledge while building rapport, engagement, and encouraging creativity among participants.[9] Ultimately, the power of "conversation" as an organizing metaphor *and* practice is that it

- focuses on language as the means for how we make the world;
- renders experience visible and available as a resource for thinking;
- structures how we talk and listen; and
- is grounded in acts of making—the language practices of conversation are a productive practice.

Situating Conversation Design

Our lens on design conversations is as interdisciplinary as our approach to LXD, though we are anchored to rhetoric as a design art. Our approach to designing conversations varies based on project needs, team readiness, and scaffolding demands. We've learned from theoretical and pragmatic frameworks on conversations, which include constructivism and linguistics, change management, and design sprint methodologies. When we design for conversations, we rely on multiple techniques from domains of expertise like cybernetics and conversation analysis (social scientific understanding and analysis of interactions),[10] and from fields in the humanities and the social sciences (see introduction). Most importantly, we see conversations as themselves learning experiences that create new opportunities for our project partners. Dubberly and Pangaro describe a conversation as "a progression of exchanges among participants. Each participant is a 'learning system,' that is, a system that changes internally as a consequence of experience. This highly complex type of interaction is also quite powerful, for conversation is the means by which existing knowledge is conveyed and new knowledge is generated."[11]

To us, this means that as learning occurs through conversation about a specific topic, participants' thoughts and ideas are made explicit and new knowledge is generated as building blocks for addressing the design problem at hand. Because the goal of design is to learn, to create new understandings, our approach to conversation has three primary influences: (1) a constructivist view of our shared reality, (2) an intentional effort to embed conversations within a change management perspective, and (3) problem-solving through challenge-based learning and design sprints.

A constructivist view of reality implies that our conversations are populated and constituted by what others have said before us and by our own ways of communicating, and that language and culture provide frameworks for our experiences, for how we communicate, and for how we understand our shared reality.[12] Our stance on language and its relationship to how we make the world is essential when designing experiences, because without it, the "experience" is elusive and often impossible to articulate. Finally, a constructivist stance holds that we tend to construct reality through narratives.[13] Rhetoric, the practical art for *doing* conversation, has strong constructivist roots and shapes our practice. We engage with an approach to rhetoric that is broadly informed by a philosophically pragmatic understanding of how humans experience and make sense of the world.[14] This pragmatism is the grounding for our insistence on the power of experience in learning experience design (see chapter 1).

A constructivist view of conversations allows us to uncover how groups perceive their shared reality. As Boehm et al. put it, such a view helps us see how these conversations include "a collection of concepts, memories and reflexes colored by our personal needs, fears, and desires, all of which are limited and distorted by the boundaries of language and the habits of our history, sex and culture."[15] This is important because individuals tend to believe that the way they perceive the world is the only way—or the most logical way—in which it can be interpreted. We keep in mind that what groups need from dialogue is to create shared meaning as "a means by which we can slow down the process of thought in order to be able to observe it while it is actually occurring."[16] Slowing down thinking, making thinking visible, and then doing something new with that shared thinking is what conversation as a design practice accomplishes.

This approach requires a bit of back and forth among participants. We accept that design is inherently grounded in argumentation, and thus "requires conversation, so that participants may understand, agree, and collaborate, all toward effective action. Not so that we can say, 'Wow, we know what's going on!,' but rather, 'Wow, we're getting somewhere, we're improving things!' We are seeing more and acting better."[17] We need to ensure that people get to explore individual and collective beliefs that feed an organization and shape an institution. We want them to participate in a process in which interactions

> can reveal the often puzzling patterns of incoherence that lead the group to avoid certain issues or, on the other hand, to insist, against all reason, on standing and defending opinions about particular issues. Dialogue is a way of observing, collectively, how hidden values and intentions can control our behavior, and how unnoticed cultural differences can clash without our realizing what is occurring. It can therefore be seen as an arena in which collective learning takes place and out of which a sense of increased harmony, fellowship and creativity can arise.[18]

We try to do exactly that as we intentionally co-design conversations with partners, such as using tools to visualize thinking and build common language around change processes. Conversations cannot accomplish their intended purpose of sparking innovation without an intentional effort to embed them within a change management framework (we take up change management as design in chapter 4). Ford, for example, proposes that conversations are both the medium and the product of reality construction, "within which change is a process of shifting conversations in the network of conversations that constitute organizations."[19] Change managers, thus, are responsible for the creation of conversational realities that produce actionable change. That is, effective, sustainable change is a function of communication and dialogue.

Indeed, this is another place where constructivism is useful, not just for how to understand and design conversations, but for understanding change management itself. While some of the organization change literature has adopted a constructivist view,[20] most take a more structural-functionalist view, in which a change agent's role is to align an organization to an objective reality "out there" through interventions.[21] However, if we think of organizations as constructed entities, where reality is interpreted and maintained through discourse, then it is conceivable that our knowledge of institutional reality can make sense through conversations.[22] The job of change agents, therefore, becomes to "create new realities in which people and organizations are more effective in achieving the outcomes to which they are committed."[23] At the Hub, we see ourselves as facilitators of conversations or change managers, depending on project needs and priorities. We design conversations to guide inquiry and understanding around shared educational realities, all the while striving to encourage teams to act on their change decisions and implement behavioral or programmatic intentions. As we argue in the introduction, "Institutions R Us." We make and change them through discourse.

This leads us to our third influence, the importance of problem-solving through challenge-based learning and design sprints as patterns for our work. We know that some of the greatest difficulties in producing change in higher education are complexities of the system, dedicated time for innovation, and creative execution.[24] We recognize the benefits of *slow*—of long-term research and the patience with new ideas that can certainly enable reflection and care.[25] Yet, our role within a university means that we have a preference for *quick*, which pushed us to look at industry practices around challenge-based problem-solving. This led us to companies that excel at change through structured conversations, such as the design sprint.

In the past decade, we have seen such active learning methodologies flourish within and outside the design industry, with companies like IDEO, Google, or Apple adapting design thinking and challenge-based processes to solve complex challenges. Many of the conversations we design, for example, are indebted to the Google Ventures Sprint method.[26] We were particularly interested in the design sprint methodology because it embeds design principles and phases like our own design model: discover, define, develop, and deliver. Of course, using design processes for complex problem-solving is not new. In 1992, Buchanan proposed that design thinking was a relevant approach to complex, wicked, or ill-structured problems.[27] To Buchanan (and we agree), such problems represent a "class of social system problems which are ill-formulated, where the information is confusing, where there are many clients and decision makers with conflicting values, and where the ramifications in the whole system are thoroughly confusing."[28] For the authors of *Sprint*, productivity with big challenges happens when it is coupled with a short deadline, through a balance of brainstorming, in-depth thinking, diversity in team expertise, and prototyping. They add, "we shortcut the endless-debate cycle and compress months of time into a single week" in order to collect viable data from realistic prototypes.[29] The Sprint process typically evolves over a five-day period, around

1. mapping out the problem at hand and identifying one element to focus on;
2. sketching competing solutions;
3. making decisions and turning ideas into testable hypotheses;
4. creating a realistic prototype; and
5. testing with real users.

When participants experience sprints, they focus on the pace, which is unusually quick for higher education. But we like sprinting because it enables depth. That is, carving out significant periods of time to focus on a finite set of issues with a group of colleagues enables depth of thought and conversation that simply isn't possible in the normal patterns of university work life.

An Example of the Hub at Work:
The French Program Redesign

Well-designed conversations can help people accomplish a great deal, and we continue to grow our toolbox of techniques to creatively engage with groups. For Ford and Ford, intentional change in an organization occurs via a dynamic of four types of conversation: *initiative, understanding, performance,* and *closure.*[30] Initiative conversations direct participants' attention to what could or should be done—a call for action—as a first phase of a change process. In turn, conversations for understanding focus on assertions, evidence, hypotheses, and beliefs.[31] Conversations for performance involve what Winograd and Flores call conversations for action—an interplay of directions to produce specific outcomes.[32] Finally, conversations for closure bring about an end to the change process and are reflective in nature. We often use a combination of these four types of conversation. We build on a group's initiative to address desired outcomes. We encourage understanding within the group through intentional processes that are human-centered and based on empathy. We also rely on performative conversations that encourage action, such as prototyping, and we make use of closure conversations as metacognitive and reflective moments for the group.

We think it is useful to illustrate how "conversation" is central to our design process by providing a concrete case example. One of our most effective design projects was an engagement with members of the French department, who found themselves at a crossroads—stuck, really—and needed a neutral space and facilitation to envision their strategic planning for a redesign of their degree programs.

The French department faculty at MSU was in a transition phase when they reached out to the Hub. They had conducted a review of their programs based on collected evaluations; they rethought what they wanted their programs to be like, and what they could do to attract more students; and they wanted to work out tensions between traditional views of language education and innovative ways to conceive of foreign languages in the twenty-first century. After consultation, the Hub imagined a set of three conversations over three weeks to answer the question, How might we reinvent what it means to study French at Michigan State University? The conversations were organized as follows:

> **Conversation 1:** *Intent statement with exploration map.*[33] This initial conversation was structured around the team mapping out the current status of their program (*from*) and its imagined future (*to*) and collectively crafting an intent statement ("Our intent is to move from a program that we might characterize as [insert *from* elements] to an experience that will [insert *to* elements]"). While the mapping exercise served the purpose of opening the conversation about how the team perceived their program, the intent statement solidified their common commitment for change. The intent statement then became the anchor for subsequent conversations.
>
> **Conversation 2:** *Understanding people and context.*[34] The second conversation brought the team together to conduct informal research and interviews to better understand both their context within higher education and also the needs of their learners. Gathering the team around divergent sets of data allowed them to converge toward a common agreement about the characteristics of their programs they wanted to highlight, redesign, or add to achieve their goal. That list of characteristics fed into the last conversation, organized around planning for execution.
>
> **Conversation 3:** *Backward design planning with mapping exercise.*[35] Backward design is used to trace the steps needed to accomplish an end goal. That last conversation with the team gave them space

to map out the process with an outcome (*to redesign their graduate programs*) and goals (*their intent statement from Conversation 1*) as informed by their context and the people involved in it (*students, faculty, administration, partners*). By working backward and discussing the steps necessary for their work, they were able to produce a clear timeline of action and anticipate potential administrative hurdles along the way.

The team continued meeting on a weekly basis to change course goals and accomplish their planned outcomes to redesign their graduate programs. Feedback from two key participants in the design conversations revealed the benefits of these interactions along three elements:

- *Space.* The Hub represented a "third space" for the team. It was a space associated specifically with curriculum work for that specific project. Even though they are located in the same building as we are, the Hub provided a physical and mental space for connecting with the project. They continued meeting in that space after our facilitation was over to work on implementing their project, which demonstrates how they saw the Hub as a space dedicated to change and motivation for innovation.
- *Activities.* Using design activities to make thinking visible (white boards, sticky notes, mapping, etc.) provided a visible consensus for the team, where they could "see" their agreements and disagreements. These activities helped them think big and not limit themselves, but the activities also helped them realize that things could change because the activities allowed them to project themselves in the imagined future version of their new programs. Having the whole team participate helped solidify ideas and suggestions.
- *Facilitation.* The Hub represented a neutral party with an assigned role and explicit structure for a conversation in which the team could focus on the conversation itself, not monitoring time, taking notes, or tending to other housekeeping matters. The team saw the facilitator enabling them to (a) stay on track

by managing time, redirecting tangents, or leveling participation of all team members; (b) figure out where to start and allowing the team to move toward execution; and (c) ask relevant questions from an outsider's perspective.

In that academic year, both their redesigned MA and PhD programs were approved by the university. In addition, they continued their redesign and started a similar process for their BA degree.

The conversations we designed with the French faculty had value because they helped those seeking change to focus on communication to construct reality and to render experiences visible and available as a resource for thinking. Language structures how we might talk and listen and is grounded in acts of making, and so facilitated conversations transform language exchanges into productive, action-oriented practices. The three elements highlighted in the case above (space, activities, and facilitation) are useful for designing conversations for innovation in higher education. Each of these elements requires careful planning, consideration, and, more importantly, relationship building, in order to achieve change in academic settings through design conversations.

Space, Activities, and Facilitation

Providing a space for teams to have design conversations is an important element to orchestrate. As the authors of *Sprint* argue, a dedicated space can act as a team's spatial and visual memory aid as members manipulate sticky notes, draw diagrams, or discuss ideas verbally.[36] A third space, like the Hub, helps groups work better together through a shared understanding that is physically and synchronously built. Ideally, a space built for purposes such as this has large wall surfaces and whiteboards for maps, research notes, sketches, or storyboards and flexible furniture to accommodate different work modes. In the case presented above, the team members involved in the French redesign were explicit about the need for a third space to disrupt the everyday patterns of their thinking. Interestingly, the Hub space was only a few hallways away from the French Department, but the team shared with us that the walk to the Hub prepared them mentally for those conversations. Furthermore, the Hub was *the* space for working on their design project. They only worked on this project in our space. The space allowed them to leave every other worry, thought, or looming deadline at the door.

Obviously, a space like the Hub is not always available, but the principles of space, visibility, and flexibility remain. This was especially relevant for the Hub as we adapted our design conversations and design sprints during the COVID-19 pandemic. It was imperative for us to provide teams with a sense of connection without the physical space that had served us so well before. In a sense, as Smith highlights in his work on design sprints for Facebook, "the more crucial deliverable, especially right now, is the shared experience."[37] In order to replicate the connectivity and engagement we have witnessed in the past, we now rely on online whiteboard tools and video conferencing. They're not ideal, but they are functional. We emphasize our use of icebreakers and informal communication to build trust and create an environment where teams can share their ideas and still feel included. This is more important than ever because at their core, design conversations are about group problem-solving, which includes disagreement and conflicts.

Physical and digital spaces are key to our practice, but "space" has psychological and emotional dimensions as well (we think about this in terms of the rhetoric of space). Part of creating a space for design conversations, whether in person or online, is to think ahead with regard to potential conflicts in order to create space for conflict as moments of growth and to avoid the destructive potential of conflict.[38] By creating specific conditions, or "third spaces," for design conversations, we are able to mitigate interpersonal group dynamics as well as build a relationship of trust and communication in order to achieve the group's design goals. We also accomplish this, in addition to creating a space for conversation, by focusing the team's interaction on actionable communication for critical and creative problem-solving.

Space for reflection is essential, but so is pivoting from reflection to action. By using design thinking activities, sticky notes, analog or digital whiteboards, and other materials, we allow groups and individuals to visualize their thinking processes. Cross frames it quite well:

> Designing, it seems, is difficult to conduct by purely internal mental processes; the designer needs to interact with an external representation. The activity of sketching, drawing or modeling provides some of the circumstances by which a designer puts him-or herself into the design situation and engages with the exploration of both the problem and its solution. There is a cognitive limit to the amount of complexity that can be handled internally; sketching provides a temporary, external store for tentative ideas, and supports the "dialogue" that the designer has between problem and solution.[39]

When talking about designing learning experiences with teams, it is important to create a common foundation (personas, scenarios, landscape analysis, goals, principles, and so on) and an intent statement as an objective and outcome for a conversation. As the team visually builds what could be called a mini design brief, facilitators are able to start conversations with a visible display of

1. a summary of the challenge space and/or purpose of the design;
2. key users;
3. main scenarios in which the solution would be used;
4. established outcomes or goals for the solution; and
5. design principles to follow.[40]

As we think about conversations as *action*, a key practice in the French project was sketching, because "sketching is literally externalized thought, which we can throw out, revise, or use as a point of discussion."[41] Different types of diagrams or mapping techniques serve that purpose (e.g., alignment diagrams, experience maps, journey maps, mental model diagrams, spatial maps, service blueprints). For the French team, alignment was key. Alignment diagrams enable visualizations of the story of interactions between individuals and units in an organization in a single overview. They also provide a common picture built on empathy and perspective-taking while reducing complexity and highlighting opportunity spaces.[42] For the French team, sketching the steps necessary to accomplish their tasks allowed them to work backward from their objective and to collaboratively build a visual timeline of actions in order of importance. Later actions included prototyping, which is typical of any design process and important for our practice as well. A curriculum or program prototype looks different from, say, a new running shoe prototype, but each helps reinforce principles of actionable conversations and allows teams to take their solutions into the world and get swift feedback. Wendt argues that actions such as this take ideas and "then extends [them] into the spaces where it really matters, creating a layer of praxical knowledge."[43] The team of French faculty was able to move quickly and capably from ideation to action, and that rhythm and the satisfaction they took in the process of creation was sustaining for them.

Throughout design conversations, but especially in the early stages, a facilitator helps shape the context of dialogue. Facilitation is conversation design in action. This was one of the main reasons the French department contacted us in the first place: their previous redesign conversations had come to dead ends. They needed an outside voice to guide their efforts to accomplish their goal in a timely manner. There are a few ways we could have approached facilitation. *Interventionists* understand facilitation in terms of keeping conversations on course— quite actively, as the name implies. With this approach, interactions between participants are guided by attention to an external authority (the facilitator), and therefore the facilitator is understood to be an outsider to the group, with a limited ability to fully participate.[44] *Noninterventionists*, which is our typical approach (although we can be interventionists), see facilitation as co-constructed. The facilitator role is to build a team-based social relationship and to act in ways consistent with constructivist notions of working to build a shared reality in that team, around shared purpose, values, respect, and perhaps most importantly, hope.[45] A facilitation approach such as this was used with our colleagues in French in an effort to build cohesion within the team, change the conversational patterns by introducing a new team member (Hub facilitator), and from there, avoid the dead ends of their past. What the French case illustrates for us is the importance of space, the preference for action, and the role of intentional facilitation approaches to enable a successful design conversation. These are design patterns that are effective, and not just for situations like the French department. And they are repeatable. And they are repeatable in part because they are theoretically grounded.

The Big Threats to Conversation Design

As we have refined our approach to designing conversations about learning experiences, we have come to identify and attend to several challenges, which include addressing issues of diversity, equity, inclusion, design fixation, and resistance to change. These issues are distinct but not mutually exclusive, and they are, needless to say, not the only challenges we face or will continue to face in the future. But they are the biggies. We are pretty sure that these issues are not unique to us, and so are worth discussion as we close this chapter.

One of the main facilitator roles is to compose the group that will participate in the design conversation. Ensuring that our conversations enable equitable interactions and are inclusive is extremely challenging. We know from any number of literatures that difference can and should lead to better outcomes.[46] Or, as Lorenzo et al. note, organizations open to contributions from all and that provide an environment that allows employees to share their ideas are more effective at fostering innovation than those that do not.[47] While we believe that diversity leads to more ethical and productive outcomes, we are also aware that inequalities and power dynamics that are often more visible in diverse groups can shape conversations in ways that are not productive. In higher education, these dynamics are commonly manifested through implicit biases around status, hierarchy, or expertise and are sometimes reinforced by us.

Acknowledging barriers to conversation within a team is critical. For instance, the Stanford d.School adapted its model in 2016 to promote equity. They added "notice" and "reflect" nodes to their process to help designers develop their own social-emotional awareness and embed a transparent reflective modality. Similarly, the Equity Design Collaborative created a framework to "make visible our individual biases; push us past the individual to the institutional, systemic, and historic inequity at play; and fight against hegemonic ideologies," a framework that addresses equity by

- designing at the margins (both the privileged and the marginalized build innovative solutions together instead of the privileged designing for the marginalized);
- embedding identity in the process (being aware of our own lenses for the world when engaging in design);
- inverting power structures (sharing power in the interest of everyone);
- making the invisible visible (highlighting the preexisting schemas governing relationships); and
- focusing on the future (creating space for ambiguity and change for purposeful new structures).

Many other design organizations are leading the way to mitigate inequities and question the status quo in design conversations. While using a human-centered design approach at the Hub was a step in the right direction, we know that *who* the humans are and *how* they are able to participate require constant vigilance. We've found that creating psychological safety through trust and respect has allowed us to build environments that are safe for interpersonal risk-taking. Relying on participatory inquiry approaches to guide how we design conversations also reminds us to privilege those most impacted by design decisions. In addition, we have come to appreciate how design sprints can help combat equity concerns when used in a way that gives everyone a voice in the conversation, including anonymous feedback on ideas when appropriate. Issues of equity don't disappear and must be accounted for in the design of conversations. We need to be held accountable as the designers of those conversations.

In addition to the challenges of diversity, equity, and inclusion, another challenge we face is a rush toward fixed design solutions, which, in our experience, is the quickest way to kill a design process. "Design fixation" or "solutionism" is neither new nor unconventional but rather a natural feature of the human mind to rely upon easily accessible and preexisting schemas for problem-solving.[48] Finding solutions quickly is undoubtedly an advantage in our evolutionary makeup, but in the case of design conversations, solutions are facets of innovation that we try to slow down, push back, or even eliminate during initial stages of the process. Quick solutions can often shut down conversations. The problem, of course, is that we often do not recognize when we are fixated on a solution, as we often see *our* idea as obviously good. Without a facilitator who can help highlight this process, team conversations often lead to "design-by-committee" or "frankensteining" ideas that combine all ideas within one design without clear attention to the objectives or goals for that design.[49] This often happens, as Crilly explains, because of exposure to prior solutions, low budgets, believing that first solutions are better, cultures of blame, or pushy stakeholders.[50] The list of threats is long and lethal.

In some conversations—and very often in the discourse patterns of higher education—people tend to argue in favor of their fixed position to convince others to change, which does not give rise to anything creative.[51] The more powerful the person or the voice, the more argument is a process killer. Our understanding of this phenomenon is why our term of art is "conversation" and not "argumentation." To circumvent these issues in the design conversations we facilitate, we have established three procedures that help groups navigate the tension between problem and solution in creative ways.

First, as we have offered, language matters tremendously in how participants are primed to view problem-solving, so we tend to use words that are more agile and flexible than *solutions* and instead, talk about *approaches* or *prototypes*. Second, addressing a group's fears early on helps people pull back from investing in their solutions (or any solution) too quickly, or at all. For example, a conversation for creativity needs to acknowledge the fears, limitations, and boundaries from the outset to free space for divergent thinking. Third, it is extremely important to spend time in the problem space to understand the problem itself. As Wendt has argued about this "problem solution paradox," we cannot think about solutions until we understand the problem, and we cannot understand a problem until we think about solutions.[52]

These three procedures are visible in the conversation patterns that we tailor to specific teams or problem spaces. This includes working on morphological charts or other mapping activities to visually identify fixations on a design or emphasizing the importance of prototyping to see the design in more material form. One of the most successful ways to address design fixation in our work has been through analogical observations. Both Linsey et al. and Moreno et al. recommended overcoming design fixation through analogical inspiration, or design-by-analogy in problem-framing.[53] Analogical examples, particularly early on in design conversations, can help a group open their minds to how other industries or organizations in completely different domains address the same problem. It may seem counterintuitive or counterproductive to turn to amusement parks to think about online learning experiences, but observing how popular franchises in that industry leverage technology and experience design to engage customers can actually benefit a team's conversation around similar approaches in higher education.

Acknowledging and addressing design fixation is an opportunity to build deeper relationships in a space of psychological safety. We attend to resistance and interpersonal conflicts within design conversations in the same manner. Resistance to change and conflict are often natural byproducts of the process involved in design conversations.[54] Resistance in conversations around new designs can happen for many reasons: threats to the status quo; anxiety about consequences, real or imagined; threats to ability to perform; or because the conversation itself asks people to question their worldview.[55] Sometimes this resistance is bigger than the problem or opportunity itself—when there is distrust or historical resentment toward the change agent, when participants understand or assess the situation differently, or when they are protecting social relationships.[56] O'Connor represents resistant behaviors as a set of types:

- The saboteur: covert and conscious, these resistors undermine change while pretending to support it
- The survivor: covert and unconscious, these resistors do not realize they are undermining change
- The zombie: covert and unconscious, these resistors are an extreme version of the survivor
- The protester: overt and conscious, these resistors believe that their refusal to change is a positive contribution to the organization[57]

In higher education and other hierarchical systems, we know that there is a "fear of expressing thoughts that might be seen as critical of those who are higher in the organization or of norms within the organizational culture."[58] This often leads to reaction-based feedback, which is driven by a person's understanding of what they are expected to say, cultural norms, or a desire to share with others what the individual thinks they want to hear.[59] We have observed most of these behaviors and understand them as normal and part of what we need to work through to build relationships with stakeholders. Our approach is far from perfect, but we have observed that focusing on transparency, openness, spontaneous curiosity, and a genuine interest in others has mitigated issues and created a safe space for them to be expressed and acknowledged. Like Ford, Ford, and McNamara, however, we see resistance to change as a constructed reality in which people are reacting to the background conversations that they perceive as driving the conversation rather than the conversation (and potential change) itself.[60] A background conversation is the "implicit, unspoken 'backdrop' or 'background' against which explicit, foreground conversations occur; it is both a context and a reality."[61] Our constructivist perspective assumes that reality is not the same for everyone, and therefore resistance is a function of a complex constructed reality, with both personal and social features, which shapes how people act. The power of conversation as a language practice, then, is "the ability to bring background constructions (assumptions, conclusions, decisions, etc.) into the foreground so that they can be examined."[62] When successful, we are able to transform frustrations into something positive.

In many ways, this chapter represents the culmination of years of observing the facilitation of successful as well as failed design conversations. Our experiences themselves have been shaped by what we bring to the design work intellectually. We have used this chapter to make those conceptual commitments and frameworks explicit, not simply because they shape how we see and understand design work but because we have turned those intellectual commitments into a design stance. We design conversations, which means that we design patterns for others to use to solve problems and realize opportunities. We do so because we believe in the power of conversations

1. to focus on language as a way to construct reality;
2. to render experiences visible and available as a resource for thinking;
3. to structure how we might talk and listen; and
4. to ground teams in acts of making.

Sometimes design conversations are productive and pleasant; at other times they are much less so. We have long accepted that design is an iterative, ambiguous, sometimes discouraging, and sometimes joyful process. We see design conversations as a key practice in our theory of change. These conversations are of tremendous value. Prompting change and creativity through design conversations is not just work; it is the work.

4

Change Management as Design

NEARLY EVERYTHING WE DISCUSS in this book is about managing change. Chapter 3, for instance, illustrates how we enable change through conversation design. It doesn't matter much if we are focused on working with individual faculty, or if we turn our gaze to organizational or institutional issues, however. In each case, we're in the change management business. In this chapter we focus on organizational issues and argue for thinking of change management as a matter of design. More to the point, we think the most effective and sustainable changes in higher education will result from design inquiries.

We are interested in moving the language around change in higher education from one of "management" to "design" because such a move helps contextualize design's role in producing change. Indeed, if we are to deal with what Bruce Mau has called the "massive change that seems to be characteristic of our time," then "we all need to think like designers."[1] Deborah Rowland urges organizations to move from "change" to "changing," from nouns to verbs.[2] This move signals the importance of building capacity for change and actions (organizational, cultural, psychological). As Rowland describes it, "in one sense, the primary task of top leaders is no longer to come up with the definitive grand plan for the future, but to create the capacity for ongoing innovation."[3] Such a shift entails a fundamental move from "what" to "how." That is, it is no longer sufficient for leadership to determine what the change will be and point the way for others to follow. *How* teams and organizations get from A to B is where leadership must dwell. A move from a top-down leadership approach to a distributed view of design leadership allows us to see change through the following lenses:

- Change is a design outcome rather than a management input.
- Change management should be designed rather than applied.
- Change carries institutional values through design leadership.

A design ethos asks us to apply systems thinking to problems, develop a deep understanding of users and their experiences, and acknowledge the value of inclusion while leveraging the contributions and involvement of others through stakeholder engagement. Given our orientation to design and organizational change, this chapter proceeds simply. We describe the modalities of change management in their current form before unpacking why we approach change management in terms of design. As we have throughout this book, we blend relevant scholarly and practice-focused work. The short version of our argument goes something like this: organizational change is something that happens when people are focused on designing something new.

What Is Change Management?

Baseline understandings of change management are well-established, both in the scholarly literature and, just as importantly, in the professional literature, which guides most change management practice. Research fundamentals in the field are grounded in disciplines such as organizational psychology and management science. Researchers work to understand the various cognitive, affective, incentive-based, and technological variables that impact how individuals and organizations understand changes to processes, roles, organizational structures, work patterns, and technologies that either drive or are part of any organizational change process.

Historically, this body of work can be traced to Kurt Lewin's three-step model of change.[4] Known as the *unfreezing-change-refreeze* process, it has dominated Western theories of organizational change for the past fifty years and influences innovation practices to this day.[5] Lewin's foundational change theory was accompanied by three additional pillars:

1. Field theory (the patterns of interaction between individuals and their environment)
2. Group dynamics (the system of behaviors and psychological dynamics within and between social groups)
3. Action research (a collaborative inquiry process that merges problem-solving actions with data-driven interactive research)[6]

The issues identified in these pillars will be visible in our discussion in this section. One of the key ideas not listed above, however, is the importance of strong leadership. As many have argued, producing change depends on the commitment of top management, the type of intervention used, people's readiness for change, the level of resistance, and the organization's culture.[7] Writing on change in institutions of higher education, for example, James Paul Gee explains that

> since institutions are frozen in thought, they often freeze a solution to a problem. The solution was good originally but gets to be less and less good as circumstances (and the problem) change. Once a solution is frozen, it takes lots of work to unfreeze it, to get people to rethink it and refreeze ("institutionalize") a different solution. Even if it can be unfrozen, it unfreezes slowly and only with much effort and controversy. People become used to the frozen solution. They take it for granted. Sometimes they have invested a lot of time and effort in learning to follow it. Sometimes they feel it was sanctioned by "higher authority" that ought not to be challenged.[8]

"Freezing" is a legitimate problem. Accordingly, much of the practice-based literature is focused on preparing an organization for change in order to "unfreeze" it. For example, one of the most commonplace contemporary frameworks, from the consultancy Prosci, has the acronym ADKAR (awareness, desire, knowledge, ability and reinforcement), which focuses on three levels of change readiness: individual, organizational, and enterprise. In order to help "unfreeze" an organization, in other words, it is necessary to raise awareness, desire, and so on.

These layers of change readiness and management are visible in the scholarly literature as well. A journey into the organizational psychology literature offers a body of work on individual and team dynamics as they impact organizations. A trip through the virtual stacks of management and strategy journals tends to produce organizational and enterprise-level inquiries. Meanwhile, the interdisciplinary contemporary leadership literature is squarely focused on leading and managing change by drawing on a broad scholarly literature. This literature has been influential for our own work at the Hub. As a whole, the literature is clear that managing change is a core competency of any organization, not a nice-to-have attribute. Yet, very few institutions of higher education are explicit about this core competency.

Todnem's review of the change management literature begins with making this core competency clear, quoting Graetz's argument that, "against a backdrop of increasing globalisation, deregulation, the rapid pace of technological innovation, a growing knowledge workforce, and shifting social and demographic trends, few would dispute that the primary task for management today is the leadership of organisational change."[9] While commonplace, Todnem notes that this leadership isn't commonly successful, citing studies that report a failure rate as high as 70 percent.[10] Even those who disagree with that number agree it's difficult to understand *why* this is the case. Is it a function of poor research? Or a function of other mediating factors that are not accounted for in these studies? Or is it caused by practices that are often based on received assumptions about how organizations work, which can easily lead to guidance that might not be well grounded or, ultimately, effective? Todnem writes that, while there is little consensus in the literature that might satisfactorily answer the "why" questions and usefully inform practice, there is widespread consensus that the pace of change in organizations is growing and that the pace is driven by internal as well as external factors.

Todnem's review provides three categories intended to describe patterns interesting to change management researchers and practitioners:

1. The rate of occurrence and its relationship to team and organizational effectiveness (Is the rate of change discontinuous or incremental?)
2. How change happens (individual, team, organizational, and so on)
3. How change comes about (models and planning frameworks)

The third category, which concerns conceptual and planning models, is what most people think about when they use the language of change management. Perhaps the most foundational model is provided by John Kotter.[11] His eight stages of change can be found everywhere:

1. Create a sense of urgency
2. Build a guiding coalition
3. Form a strategic vision and initiatives
4. Enlist a volunteer army
5. Enable action by removing barriers
6. Generate short-term wins
7. Sustain acceleration
8. Institute change

The ADKAR model and process that we introduced earlier (awareness, desire, knowledge, ability, and reinforcement) is similar to Kotter's work and no doubt builds on it (both are susceptible to the critique that they are linear and top down—more on this later). To provide another example of how to think about change, Anderson and Anderson's leadership-focused accountability model attends to four key issues (mindset, behavior, culture, and systems) that are relevant to managing change.[12] These issues scale from the individual to the organizational. Each of these approaches—and there are more, to be sure—have several things in common: (1) mindset (internal, individual), (2) culture (internal, collective), (3) behavior (external, individual), and (4) systems (external, collective).

First, change management approaches are grounded in an underlying psychology concerned with motivation (fear? urgency? reward?) and in the importance of how that underlying psychology impacts individual and team mindsets. To change an organization, individuals' mindsets need to be understood and adapted. Second, these practice-focused models are attentive to organizational culture and strategy. To change an organization requires that one respect and work with the existing culture, and no change in that culture is possible without a clear organizational or business strategy. Finally, each approach respects the power of process as the mode of execution. Without effective processes, there is no instituting change or reinforcing new modes of operation. As Factor elaborates,

> no organization wants to be subverted. No organization exists to be dissolved. An organization is, by definition, a conservative institution. If you didn't want to conserve something, why would you organize? Even if an organization runs into serious trouble—if, perhaps, its market or reason for existence vanishes—there remains a tremendous resistance to change. (And, by the way, our larger culture is also an organization.) I suggest that the most one can hope for is a change in the more superficial elements which would naturally occur as an organization co-opts . . . some of dialogue's ethic of inquiry. And maybe that is all that is required to accomplish its aims. But any deeper change, any change that might threaten the very meaning and therefore the existence of the organization or its power relations would tend to be rejected—perhaps subtly and tacitly—because such vulnerability would not only be threatening to those within the group, but almost certainly to those who perceive from without—perhaps from higher up the corporate ladder—what this sub-grouping of their organization is getting up to.[13]

What we've shared so far about models for managing change will be familiar to those who have studied or been part of change management work. Kotter's ideas ground much management and leadership advice.[14] But despite a seemingly solid ground, change management doesn't seem to work as often as we would like. It's very likely that the failure to effectively execute organizational change may be a function of faulty understandings of change management as planned. Orlikowski and Hoffman warned nearly twenty-five years ago that "today . . . given more turbulent, flexible, and uncertain organizational and environmental conditions, such a [planned] model is becoming less appropriate."[15] Indeed, one way to understand the critique of historical understandings of change management and their contemporary practical applications is in terms of a shift from *planned* in favor of *emergent* approaches to managing change.

Planned approaches are what Graetz and Smith characterize as "a formulaic approach which pre-supposes that organizational change can and should be a controlled and orderly affair, a simple case of 'unfreezing,' 'moving' and 'refreezing.'"[16] In contrast, Todnem writes that "the emergent approach to change emphasizes that change should not be perceived as a series of linear events within a given period of time, but as a continuous, open-ended process of adaptation to changing circumstances and conditions."[17] This provides us with the language of continuous change and the need for organizations to become learning organizations so that they can be culturally and practically capable of adaptation. These are important ideas for the argument that managing change is a core competency and to our argument that design is an optimal pathway for executing change. Indeed, there is much overlap in terms of how *planned* and *emergent* approaches understand the nature of organizations and how organizations (and people) change. Change is almost always emergent *and* planned. The choice of which approach is more appropriate is driven by how participants understand their organization and context. Therefore, readiness and the ability to facilitate in a context of considerable individual, interpersonal, and systems complexity emerge as more important to the effectiveness of any given change process than the rough distinction between planned or emergent change.

Readiness is critical to change management. Weiner's consideration of change readiness is exceptionally useful because, as an implementation scientist, he is interested in execution, particularly the conditions that are necessary for execution.[18] Readiness is commonly understood as an individual and team resolve or commitment characterized by a set of complex dynamics (emotional, psychological, experiential, technical). Weiner's focus is psychological in nature, not structural, though the theory he proposes in this particular article is intended to knit together the two. That is, readiness is fundamentally a feature of individual and team mindsets, not an organizational feature. Yet structural and systemic issues, understood as braided with individual and team readiness, set the scene for any organizational change. As he argues, "resources and other structural attributes of organizations do not define or indicate readiness. Instead, they function as determinants of one facet of organizational readiness: change efficacy."[19] He also offers that "change commitment and change efficacy—the two facets of organizational readiness—are conceptually interrelated and often empirically correlated. Lack of confidence in one's capabilities to execute a course of action can impair one's motivation to engage in that course of action."[20]

Change commitment and efficacy tend to move in the same direction. As Ajzen highlights in his *Theory of Planned Behavior*, in order for the implementation of change intentions to be successful, it is necessary to identify the factors (attitudes, norms, self-efficacy) that might represent barriers at the individual and organizational levels.[21] In our work with teams on campus, we certainly have noticed the complex and intricate relationship between these elements and the change management work we have attempted to execute, sometimes unsuccessfully, in the projects we lead. Understanding the level of readiness between and among the people in a project is one of our most complex tasks and a source of considerable struggle and failure for us. Very little design and change in higher education is possible without the fact or cultivation of readiness for change.

It is safe to say that we have a complicated relationship with the change management literature and an even more complicated relationship with our experiences of change management in practice. When treated as a variation of project management, change work is too often linear, narrowly outcome-driven, top down, and technical (what Graetz and Smith might describe as the rational change model, which still predominates).[22] We know top-down urgency can ring hollow. Deep participation and conversation are easy to skip, shorten, and otherwise stunt. Yet our discussion here is not meant as a critique of change management per se, as we see ourselves as change managers. It is also true that there is much in the professional change management literature to guide us. Even in higher education, which can seem stable and unchanging—"frozen"—we maintain that change is continuous, not periodic, episodic, or generational.

Our claim that change is continuous is fundamental to the argument of the book and how we operate. Our ability to respond to the need for continuous change is cultural. So, any change management work in higher education must build and cultivate a culture that enables it. This book has focused completely on *how* questions, and this chapter is no different. We propose that what is required is an approach to facilitating change. That process must be inclusive, participatory, and in these ways, more effectively sustainable. Not surprisingly, we believe that this stance toward change management is a design stance and that design provides a viable, if not optimal, inquiry and planning framework for facilitating change in higher education. We unpack this belief by focusing on a case that helped us develop our approach to change management as project-oriented and grounded in design.

Design as Implicit Agent of Change

Perhaps we should critique change management just a bit. The "rational-change" model that Graetz and Smith argue predominates in much of the scholarship and nearly all of the professional literature is grounded loosely in the notion that both individuals in an organization and the organization itself are "rational actors"—choices are freely and explicitly made, based on visible and well-understood motivations and criteria—and on the notion that change can and should be managed. As Graetz and Smith see it, "with stability and control the end goals, rational models represent a singular, partial story told by senior management and consequently ignore the many other distinctive stories unfolding around them in the organizational narrative."[23] As an example of a "rational actor" process, Anderson and Anderson write about change management in terms of "change infrastructures," which include "standard roles, templates, and methods for governing your change initiatives, as well as common practices for setting up, orchestrating, and overseeing their effectiveness."[24] Quite contrary to this, Graetz and Smith argue that "understanding change as part of a continuing work in progress calls for a much broader canvas that seeks out competing voices, and works with the resulting ambiguities, contradictions and tensions of messy reality."[25] They call for "a paradigmatically different sort of philosophy . . . [which] captures the complexities and dynamics of organizations and actively seeks out the accumulated knowledge, skills, experience and learning of the different communities interacting in them."[26] If we follow this critique, and we do, then effective, sustainable change management isn't an N-step process or particularly linear and rational. It is much more complex, ambiguous, messy, and not easily managed from the top.

We know institutional change is possible, particularly if we work in a participatory way in those "zones of ambiguity," which we noted in the introduction are often found within the processes of decision-making, those rhetorical moments and systems that form the very structure of the institution itself. We can operate in those zones, and sometimes we can also *create* them by designing new processes for people to talk, listen, act, and confront differences (see chapter 3, on conversations). In this regard, we argue for approaching change management as a design challenge. We see organizational change as fundamentally "emergent," not "planned," as something that is possible when readiness is heightened in a positive, nonthreatening way, and as implicit—as something that happens along the way to something else.

The notion that organizational change happens on the way to something else is a powerful idea. As we noted in our introduction, the intrinsic value of design is sometimes more important than explicit goals, including organizational change. As such, the implicit value and associated outcomes are more important than any products: "In other words, value is inherent in the means, rather than the ends. Such values include social cohesion, ideological coherence, and strategic alignment that emerge from participation in design activities."[27] This suggests that organizational change as emergent is possible because of the ways an organization routinely behaves. This is true in our experience. An organization is what it does because culture lives in behavior. We know an organization not by its organizational chart but by how people act. This is fundamentally why the most lasting and impactful changes in an organization are going to come from the bottom up, from a thoughtful and participatory process. And they are likely going to come when organizational change per se isn't on the table. People like the idea of change and innovation, but they rarely like to be the ones who change. This is one reason why, as Deserti and Rizzo argue, "established organizations naturally develop a resistance to change," especially when a value and outcome like "innovation" is introduced at a moment of significant uncertainty or framed as a "last chance" to be faced at a moment of crisis.[28]

We suggest that the pathway to sustainable and effective change management in higher education is through design, which requires a design culture (though we can work miracles when a team simply adopts a design mindset). That culture needs to enable strategic efforts that are core to the business of the department, college, or unit rather than focusing on changing the business structurally or systematically.[29] To illustrate what we mean, let's stay with Deserti and Rizzo, who are also interested in how design challenges change management as a "prescriptive and top-down practice, in which organizational models and their sets of techniques and tools are normally abstracted from a context, operationalized, and transferred and applied to other contexts."[30] Design, they argue, challenges "the natural organizational attitudes of preservation and resistance to change, generating a constant tension between the search for innovation and the necessity of relying on established ideas and solutions," and it can "introduce a bottom-up perspective to organizational change that usually takes place in unexpected ways during the development of new products within companies."[31] Their article reports on a study of these very issues. They examined new product development processes that

- forced the employees to overcome their limits and dogmas;
- aligned the employees with the potential of a new vision;
- encouraged the companies to transform the processes of production, distribution, and communication; and
- helped the companies revise their strategies and develop their own design culture.[32]

The initiatives they studied focused on product development and not precisely on changing a struggling organization. They note the following outcomes:

> This attention [to design thinking] resulted in the adoption of a set of techniques and tools in the field of idea generation that managers are supposed to learn and easily replicate in different contexts because thinking in a designerly way could be the key to creating and fostering innovation. Such tools and techniques reflect a serious misunderstanding: Design does not contribute to innovation simply by generating new ideas; it does so by actually constructing new, viable solutions. This construction can occur only in environments characterized by a real design culture, as we defined it, through new product development processes that are likely to introduce or require concurrent organizational changes. Thus, the real innovation booster that could radically change companies, competencies and processes, and even transform people in organizations lies in managing innovation projects using a situated design culture.[33]

That last sentence is the kicker. The real innovation booster is managing projects using a situated design culture. We know this from so many other contexts. The impact of a design culture in some of the most influential companies, such as Apple or IBM, is well documented.[34] So, sure, organizational change happens on the way to other things (like new product development), *but only if we have a situated design culture.* How many higher education institutions have a situated design culture? Very few, which is one reason we wrote this book.

The relationships between design and change management are more complicated still, and to illustrate this, we turn to this chapter's case. The case focuses on one of our first projects, curriculum reform in veterinary medicine. This is the only project that sits in both our "success" and "failure" files. It is a rich resource for describing the complexities of change management, and the case will also put pressure on our own argument that organizational change is something that happens on the way to something else.

When Change Doesn't Happen: Curriculum Reform in Veterinary Medicine

The College of Veterinary Medicine (CVM) Curriculum Redesign Project was a three-year, exceptionally complex project. In many ways, the effort is the sort of project an organization like the Hub was created to address. Curriculum reform in Veterinary Medicine was one of the inaugural Hub projects. We cut our teeth on this project, taking it on before we were ready. It started in the summer of 2016 and involved three distinct phases. The overall goal of the project was to help CVM address student learning (and ideally student debt) by way of a complete curriculum redesign. The goal was to "produce a better day-one ready-veterinarian" in less time. Essential in the curriculum redesign effort was attention to the cultural shifts and change management processes necessary to support CVM faculty working differently.

Project Description

In *Phase I* of the College of Veterinary Medicine curriculum redesign, based on initial discovery work and a scan of the field, we began the process of envisioning what a competency-based education (CBE) framework might look like within veterinary education. Faculty identified initial competencies, subcompetencies, and learning outcomes ("descriptors") that would align with the national competency framework provided by the Association of Veterinary Medical Colleges (AAVMC). All competencies were sorted both vertically and horizontally, allowing them to be clustered according to systems and incremental skill development.

Phase II of the CVM curriculum design project included the development of twelve year-one competency-based courses, as well as the faculty development programming needed to ensure that CVM educators would be prepared to further thrive in designing and implementing a competency-based framework.

Phase III included the design of twelve Year Two courses, as well as the faculty development programming needed to ensure that CVM educators would be prepared to thrive in both designing and further implementing the competency-based framework. This phase included continuing the work on the faculty development plan for the first year curriculum. Finally, we addressed helping Vet Med sustain the effort with regard to ongoing curriculum, assessment, and professional development. Across Phase III, the Hub deliberately shifted into the background of the project as CVM took on more responsibility for sustaining project work.

Planned Objectives

Across the three phases of the project, the Hub-CVM Team focused on the following objectives:

1. *Design curriculum:* CVM faculty, with Hub consultation, will design year one and two of the program focused on active learning (aligned with AAVMC domains and competencies).
2. *Design teaching and learning community of practice:* CVM, with Hub consultation, will design and facilitate faculty learning community (FLC) sessions for years one, two, and three faculty.
3. *Design instruments for assessing student success:* CVM, with Hub consultation, will design consistent and program-wide student success assessment mechanisms and benchmarks.
4. *Design plans for ongoing implementation and sustainability:* CVM, with Hub consultation, will design a sustainability plan, program assessment plan, and curricular assessment framework for ongoing project success.

Actual Outcomes

In concluding the CVM Project, we were able to deliver a year-one competency-based curriculum and the foundations for years two and three competency-based curricula (objectives 1 and 2), a plan for continuing and sustaining production of the new courses, an educator professional development plan (objective 3), and the beginnings of an assessment program and a plan for project sustainability (objectives 4 and 5). CVM was not able to fully resource the initially planned leads structure in objective 3, a robust set of instruments for assessing student success (objective 4), or a sustainability plan (objective 5).

Implications

We were able to design and build a significant foundation for meeting the project's objectives. Yet the project did not produce its intended outcomes, and over time, the project seems to have frozen (if not regressed) where we left it. As a curriculum design project, it was successful. As a change management effort, much less so.

Implementation of the course design and production model was uneven. Forty-five percent of respondents in the class who experienced the new first-year curriculum identified a lack of organization as the biggest challenge they faced. When the course design and production model was followed, the students enjoyed the new courses and found that they supported their learning. The teams that implemented the design and production model (sticking to deadlines, aligning course objectives and activities, designing active learning) had the most positive results with students. However, a number of factors, including lack of buy-in from faculty and administrators, inability or unwillingness to clear faculty schedules to fully commit to course development, and uncertainty resulting from such a dramatic shift in teaching practice made it difficult to follow the course models consistently. As a result, students often felt frustrated and confused when experiencing the courses that didn't implement as many active elements as promised or weren't ready on time to enable quality review and revision. Teams needed to be further supported from design through implementation, including adequate faculty resourcing, incentives, and accountability mechanisms.

Leadership transitions created persistent resourcing, incentive, and cultural issues. The curriculum reinvention was one of many changes that happened at CVM during the time of the project. We saw a new dean, new department chairs, the loss of key faculty champions, and most importantly, the loss of the associate dean who had led the effort. In addition, admissions criteria shifted, changing the prerequisites expected of incoming students, which was critical given the competency-based design. The CVM clinic was understaffed during the majority of the reinvention. Few of these changes were experienced as positive, and morale in CVM dropped over time. At times, the curriculum reinvention was blamed for morale issues, causing faculty and staff concern about the effort.

While we have good, if tentative outcome data from the first year of the curriculum, the project faced a set of threats in the form of leadership issues that predated the project and became worse as time went on. At multiple points, we escalated these issues of leadership, proper resourcing, and support for faculty. We were able to free up some faculty time, provide letters for tenure and promotion files, and hire more staff. We transitioned the project before the fundamental leadership issues were resolved.

Adequately resourced educator and curriculum development over the longer-term remained uncertain. Adequate resourcing for longer-term sustainability was a persistent barrier to success. Necessary changes were needed to faculty time allotments and clinical assignments. Additional resourcing is still needed for both leadership and support staff, who are primarily focused on curriculum design and educator professional development. At the moment of transition, faculty working on the curriculum reinvention continued to voice concern that the work on this effort would not be valued when it came to their professional evaluations.

While resourcing has improved since the beginning of this project, many of the recommendations for faculty development leadership and staffing had not been followed at the time of transition. Indeed, the key faculty champions who left the university were focused on educator professional development. The lack of support for faculty change management in teaching and learning will be fatal to successful completion and sustainability for CVM.

There are a number of relevant features of this case for our discussion. First, the veterinary medicine effort began as a curriculum design project, and the entire project team, including our partners in veterinary medicine, focused narrowly on curriculum. This means that at the inception of the project—the key moment when we conceptualized the scope and secured the initial administrative buy-in—we were not focused on the totality of the change management work required. This had a number of implications over time with regard to the conversations we didn't have early in the project, particularly with chairs and a larger group of faculty in the college. Simply put, one source of error in this project was our singular focus on curriculum, combined with a lack of experience. In hindsight, we also made a number of assumptions about the state of conversation and awareness in the College of Veterinary Medicine that existed prior to our partnership with them.

Second, this project immediately touched the entire enterprise in the college in ways that surprised us, but shouldn't have. As we focused on competencies and assessment and how these fit together, participants started worrying about merit review and tenure and promotion and the status of clinical faculty in the college. None of these larger issues was in our design brief. Yet every single idea in the curriculum design touched on these issues. Questions of value and of how faculty spend their time became front and center for faculty at the moment when the time and energy required of a multiyear, complete curriculum redesign became visible. While leadership of the college wrote letters for annual review files and were confident that the work would be rewarded, faculty weren't as confident. MSU is an institution where research productivity is the primary, and in some cultures on campus, only measure that matters. While those faculty and staff most closely involved were committed to the project, the further away we moved from the core group the less the commitment and the greater the concern. Changes in clinical teaching proposed by the curriculum created a flashpoint. The college has a teaching hospital. In the best of times, the business needs of the hospital put tremendous pressure on the time allocations of faculty, who must also teach and research. The curriculum redesign destabilized that situation.

These issues of labor and value and trust, which were generated by the curriculum redesign, can be opportunities *if* they are anticipated and accounted for. That is, issues of labor and trust were problems in that college, and the curriculum design project could have been a moment to work through each of them in turn. If we were going to ask faculty to work differently because of how we wanted to educate students differently, then it is perfectly reasonable to look at the larger patterns of work and how work is valued in a way that is participatory and focused on issues of equity. But that didn't happen. In fact, as these issues emerged, we were told we couldn't put them on the table because of a third feature of this case: the executive leadership wasn't as strong as we thought it was when we began. The project was led by a strong and dynamic associate dean working for a dean in the last years of his tenure. Invisible to us in the first year of the project, but evident later, was the realization that the chairs were not all on board, something we assumed (again) but did not verify. While we have called into question the commonplace of the "strong leader" in the change management literature, we don't dismiss the critical importance of *strong leadership*, which in higher education is more a function of a coherent leadership team committed to shared values and direction than of a single person (though a strong dean or provost always helps).

Finally, this case allows us to highlight an important but perhaps subtle issue—the issue of design culture, which Deserti and Rizzo emphasize in their study. There was no design culture in Veterinary Medicine or at MSU then. The design culture at MSU is much stronger now than when we began this project, but it still isn't strong. Therefore, we had no deep well of cultural and intellectual resources to draw from as we engaged in an exciting curriculum design project that soon became a complicated change management project. What is fascinating about this project as we reflect on it (and we do so often) is the set of features we've described here. Had this project been presented as a change management project, focused on the need to change Veterinary Medicine as an organization, it would have been rejected. It was possible, however, to imagine a major curriculum change and to account for larger organizational issues as an outcome. This didn't happen, of course, but it is possible to imagine that organizational change can happen on the way to something else (curriculum redesign, in this case). To be effective, we would have had to account for these larger organizational issues in the design brief. As a consequence, the Veterinary Medicine project sits in our "successes" folder but also our "failures" folder.

Concluding More Hopefully: A Preview of an Experience Design Project That Has to Get It Right

As we write this chapter, we have initiated a design project on the first- and second-year experiences at MSU, a first for this institution. The project has clear and aligned executive leaders who are interested in "experience" as an outcome and design as a way to understand and build it. We have a real chance to leverage the design culture we have built to place human experiences first, focus on people's affective journeys, build models responding to complex challenges, prototype potential solutions, and more importantly, accept failure and transparency.[35] This effort is also quite clearly a change management effort, as the functions involved include academic programs, student services functions, housing, and so on. Because we are also focused on the digital student experience, this project has a significant technological component to it. We are hopeful and excited about this initiative, but for it to be successful, we need to keep in mind that the organizational changes are outcomes of the experience we design, and that this time we need to get the people right, especially those in positions of authority. We have a chance to learn from prior efforts.

In her book on leading mindful change, Deborah Rowland argues for understanding change as continuous and emergent in contemporary organizations and therefore for a leadership mindset that is appropriate.[36] Her stance echoes much of the review of the change management literature earlier in this chapter: change is a constant, leadership matters (differently than it has in the past), and perhaps most importantly for our purposes here, *how* an organization facilitates change is more important than the change goal.

Rowland argues to her audience of executives and would-be executives that "above all else" what they need to do is adopt "an emergent change approach in which [they] set a loose overall intention, but within that frame tear up any thought of long-term plans, or finding a single silver bullet, and instead work in a step-by-step, experimental, trial and error way."[37] This is, of course, music to our ears, as she sketches a design process focused on iteration, prototyping, and learning. She goes on to counsel that such an iterative approach to change requires deep participation across the organization ("work to join up multiple stakeholders"), a focus on key business issues that are widely understood to be important, and investment in the readiness and culture of the organization to execute change (design) processes. This is a good template for the executive leadership of the student experience design project, and we have certainly shared this information with them. They know that if we go to our colleagues and say, for example, "we need to change your program," it won't matter much what comes after the first part of that sentence. Particularly in higher education, programmatic persistence feels safe, and faculty and academic staff have learned to trust safe.[38] We have some confidence that a focus on student experience with reference to shared student success outcomes supported by a well-designed conversation might just be experienced as a safe place for participants to explore how to provide a new student experience.

Yet perhaps the biggest challenge to designing change in higher education is that we need new infrastructures and processes to support the creativity of students and faculty and to be able to lead, not simply respond to (or get run over by) the pace and scale of the demands placed on higher education. For example, MSU has partnered to offer a small number of "boot camps" in areas where we have programmatic strength but little capacity to be responsive to labor market demands and those learners who seek knowledge, skill, and credentials to respond to those demands. What has struck us about our work with our boot camp partner is how quickly they can adapt curriculum. They make changes in weeks, where it takes us at least a year, typically three, to make any adaptation to curriculum. To be sure, there is virtue in slow, and we would argue that some of what a university does should be carefully crafted over time. But slow is the only speed at which our operating system runs, and it is often willfully incurious and dismissive of learning from others. What higher education lacks as a sector is the capacity to prototype new infrastructures, processes, and experiences. Building that capacity is necessary.

5

Assessment and Research in a Higher Education Design Organization

WILLIAM F. HEINRICH and REBECCA L. MATZ

LOOKING AT CHANGE MANAGEMENT as design is one thing; measuring outcomes and impacts of these changes is another. This chapter deals with questions of assessment and research in a higher education design organization. We contend that design should be grounded in these practices, from the assessment of innovative designs that inform decision-making to the production of scholarly work that contributes to research domains. We describe approaches to assessment and research that are useful for conceptualizing problems and creating opportunities for change within a design organization. Along the way, we use a few examples to illustrate the role of assessment or research in our design work. The key takeaway is that assessment and research are vital to a design agenda that seeks to be transformative.[1]

Sometimes assessment and research are just that: ways to observe and understand the environment with the goal of developing theory and accumulating knowledge. In the Hub for Innovation in Learning and Technology, which is focused on transformation in an institution that values and rewards assessment and research, these activities have additional symbolic value. When a "third space," such as the Hub, uses familiar terms, it becomes clearer to partners that a relationship of trust and accountability—necessary for achieving a design agenda—is possible.

The skills of an investigator include the ability to frame a problem theoretically, select and justify an assessment or research design, identify and evaluate sources, place a problem in both a literature-based and local context, deploy methods to collect and analyze data, infer meaning, and communicate with peers. Design work in higher education is no different, requiring assessment and research in project scoping, implementation, and evaluation. Importantly, the researchers, scholars, and artists who can do this work are located all across, and in some cases outside, the institution, and at multiple levels of the typical academic hierarchy as well (students, faculty, and staff).

Defining Assessment and Research in a Loosely Coupled System

Often, the terms *assessment* and *research* carry a specific set of meanings in higher education (the same can be said for *evaluation*, which we won't take up here). Assessment and research with respect to student learning have different purposes in higher education yet often use similar methods, so it is useful to clarify differences between the terms as we use them here. *Assessment of* and *research on* learning are some of the more sacred ideas in the academy, so deploying these terms carefully and knowing how they work for different stakeholders is especially important when it comes to working on design across the institution. Specifically, it is important for design-driven investigators to clarify the nature of the question they're asking: Are they primarily trying to investigate phenomena and apply findings to a generalizable space (*research*)? Or are they evaluating the nature, quality, or effectiveness of a campus activity for internal purposes (*assessment*)? Reward structures aside, neither approach is more or less correct, but there are pros and cons to each.

Assessment in higher education is used at multiple scales and layers of the institution, from student learning to program assessment to assessment for accreditation. In all cases, however, assessment is focused on improving the nature of the local educational context and ulti-mately, therefore, on student learning and the student experience.[2] Linda Suskie's guide to assessing student learning identifies four steps: establish goals, create learning opportunities, systematically collect data, and use results to improve.[3] Assessment in higher education is an idea well used and understood at the student learning level yet often loathed at the institutional level by the same people. So, when we talk about assessment in our design practice, we are usually talking about a general form of assessment rather than a specific approach or instrument. We talk about the value of assessment and then about how to operationalize that value. For example, program assessment for accreditation is an important value proposition, but the value is much different from that of a well-designed assessment survey to inform and improve a student experience. If the survey is about an activity in that program, obviously the details are linked. But the ex-perience of the people we're talking to is a key factor in how we talk about assessment, adapting to the needs of our partners.

Research in higher education that supports designing and redesign-ing experiences attempts to accomplish a similar goal as *assessment*—improving the nature of a local educational context—while also speak-ing to a broader audience, with a coherent theoretical perspective and study design. Scholarly outlets such as academic journals and confer-ence presentations require, implicitly or otherwise, alignment with disciplinary norms for social and applied science research. It is, there-fore, necessary that research in support of a design agenda draw on research traditions and expertise in education and the social sciences. It is additionally necessary to draw on disciplinary knowledge for the problem at hand and from communities that identify with discipline-based education research and the scholarship of teaching and learn-ing.[4] In the midst of focusing on design, testing theory and creating new knowledge are often possible.

The Hub, and therefore its application of assessment and research, exists within a large educational institution, what Karl Weick describes as a loosely coupled system.[5] A loosely coupled system has a decentral-ized organizational structure, which supports collaborative goal setting and prioritization, adaptive responses, autonomy in work, and alignment. The system acts as an informational network, which, in turn, helps stakeholders coordinate a robust response to problems. Trust generated within the group creates an information portal for extended networks of loosely coupled campus partners, who collaborate to tackle a similarly loosely coupled set of problems. Weick describes seven functions of loose coupling that can drive organizational behaviors.

1. Loose coupling lowers the probability that the organization will have to—or be able to—respond to each little change in the environment that occurs.
2. Loosely coupled systems preserve many independent sensing elements and therefore "know" their environments better than is true for more tightly coupled systems, which have fewer externally constrained, independent elements.
3. A loosely coupled system may be a good system for localized adaptation.
4. Loosely coupled systems preserve more diversity in responding than do tightly coupled systems and therefore can adapt to a considerably wider range of changes in the environment.
5. If there is a breakdown in one portion of a loosely coupled system, this breakdown is sealed off and does not affect other parts of the organization.
6. In a loosely coupled system there is more room available for self-determination by the actors, leading to greater efficacy.
7. Loosely coupled systems seem to hold the costs of coordination to a minimum. Despite this being an inexpensive system, loose coupling is also a nonrational system of fund allocation and is, therefore, unspecifiable, unmodifiable, and incapable of being used as means of change.[6]

The university's behavior as a loosely coupled system yields both affordances and constraints for assessment and research. As an example of an affordance, the Hub is positioned in a boundary-spanning role. Faculty and staff work there, yet the Hub is not a typical academic department or unit bounded by one discipline. Administrators work there too, but the Hub is not solely an administrative entity. As described elsewhere in this book, the Hub operates as a third space on campus, a design group within a research university. This positioning within the loosely coupled system allows the Hub to be seen as a safe and creative space for those who seek it, while allowing other parts of the organization to ignore the work of the Hub and carry on with their daily activities.

In contrast, the loosely coupled nature of the system also presents challenges. For example, university actors are not always aware of the affirmative functions of loosely coupled systems or how best to exploit them. Hub staff are therefore responsible for engaging approaches that recognize and work to leverage the useful parts of these systems. Doing so helps our partners, but the Hub staff also operates without authority to make changes themselves and so must rely on relationships, networks, and taking advantage of the space left by nonsystemic planning in a loosely coupled system (the zones of ambiguity mentioned in the introduction).

The Hub uses *assessment* and *research* (among other tools) to connect loosely coupled elements within the institution. That is, assessment and research in the service of design help to provide frames that make sense of the loosely coupled system for a partner unit that is trying to effect change. Using the scaled and layered structures of assessment and research, we can better understand how the organization is linked together structurally, but also, politically, relationally, and symbolically.[7] A key challenge for the Hub is to effectively function as a boundary-spanning unit and leverage design work for good practices in the institution while subtly shifting the larger organization toward designing for the student experience in the presence of other considerable priorities (e.g., research).

Finally, it is important to understand a large university as a loosely coupled system because most of the partners we work with have a change mandate in hand, and we need to know how the larger system is operating around them. Working in the system allows us to best leverage its various elements and help co-design solutions for our partners. For example, sometimes a project seeks to make something obsolete that is not working in order to create space for a new, more sustainable solution. In a loosely coupled system, objectives need not always be focused on creating something new but could be thought of as removing existing barriers in order to accelerate changes. We assume that the assessment and research work is responding to a design question, giving the work a clear purpose that helps the university meet its goals to transform itself for student success. To be effective, we must first know what to do and then gain insights into how to do it.

Tactical Uses of Assessment and Research in Design Work

In any project, research and assessment are critical to success. The Hub's focus on improving student experiences, academic programs, and in some cases, the professional learning of colleagues has yielded a pattern of research and assessment approaches and methods deployed at the beginning, during, and at the end of a project. The purposes of research and assessment vary for each project but remain aligned with the improvement goals set at the beginning.

In design approaches, we often lead with a key question, which amounts to "How might we make things better for people?" This question-driven approach is aimed at preventing ourselves and our partners from leading with a solution. To understand the context of the challenge, the Hub uses a variety of assessment and research methods to help everyone understand the landscape, including stakeholder needs assessments, such as interviews, focus groups, or observations of an environment. For more contextual understanding, we might use landscape analyses, such as market research in the cases of a new or revised academic program design. These are just a few examples of methods used to understand the starting point. Design work then proceeds past stakeholder engagement to problem definition with stakeholders, ideation, prototyping, testing, and implementation. For examples of activities to help with every stage of design, a graphic from Libby Hoffman (figure 5.1) helps visualize some available methods.[8]

As a project matures and becomes more complex, two tools that

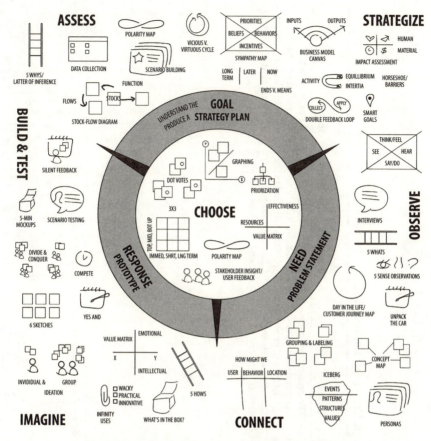

Figure 5.1. Libby Hoffman's Map of Design Methods

help with process description and assessment are a logic model and a theory of change.[9] Logic models typically follow a structure similar to those shown in table 5.1, describing resources, activities, outputs, outcomes, and impact. This simple approach helps users think through their work from start to finish or, working backward, from hoped-for outcomes to needed resources, processes, and actions that will support accomplishing the stated goals. A theory of change builds on the same processes as a logic model and, to a first approximation, adds a lot of detail. Of note, the theory of change helps detail multiple layers of activity, assumptions, and barriers to action, all of which can be evaluated. In a course or across an academic or cocurricular program,

Table 5.1. *Logic Model Program Implementation Template*

Resources	Activities	Outputs	Short- & Long-Term Outcomes	Impact
In order to accomplish our set of activities, we will need the following:	In order to address our problem or asset, we will accomplish the following activities:	We expect that, once accomplished, these activities will produce the following evidence or service delivery:	We expect that, if accomplished, these activities will lead to the following changes in 1–3 then 4–6 years:	We expect that, if accomplished, these activities will lead to the following changes in 7–10 years:

Source: W. K. Kellogg Foundation, "Logic Model Development Guide," https://www.aacu.org/node/5682, 2004.

a theory of change can help identify multiple outcomes (competencies) and multiple locations for action (courses or sets of courses). A theory of change should be built on a more general theory or framework for change (those ideas that go beyond any single project) and be more operational in nature.[10]

The efforts to detail the layers of action in a theory of change or logic model typically emerge during a prototyping phase. The tools we have mentioned here can both act as a long-range planning tool for the project itself and serve as a basis for evaluation and peer review. The theory of change makes a project visible to external stakeholders, creating accountability for quality as well as early opportunities for feedback and iterations, both important aspects of design. A well-developed theory of change is often co-constructed by us with our partner, and the act of co-creating usually yields important insights, gaps, and intellectual outcomes that improve the overall project. A theory of change then serves as a reminder of the plan, a basis for evaluation, and a way to share with new participants. It also provides one way to talk about work publicly.

Across the Hub's portfolio, staff members use a shared logic model in the form of our design process (see chapter 2 for more on that process and variations on the model). Because we integrate our process with Asana, our current project management software solution, our process functions to detail the layers of activity and effort in a project. We build in data-gathering tools to better identify pivots in the trajectory of projects, which facilitates our ability to see larger patterns and needs across projects. As a model of practice, we can evaluate practices across projects for opportunities to improve and better serve the needs of the campus.

Measuring project outcomes is an important activity across the Hub's portfolio, and it is critical when we come to the end of a project. To answer the question, "How do we know if our work has been successful, had any value, or made an impact?," we have to measure against goals. One key challenge in this work is that all the projects in the Hub's portfolio are, by design and definition, new work. Innovation presents a particular challenge because project leads and part-

Table 5.2. Hub Performance Objectives

Objective 1. Facilitate human-centered design (HCD) processes that elicit stakeholder perspectives to inform needs before seeking a solution.	*Objective 4.* Partners implement the designed learning experience, program, service, or intervention and assess measures of impact.
Objective 2. Contribute to partners' organizational transformation process and help build capacity for partners to lead future transformation. (Transformation is loosely defined as a personal or organizational identity shift that accompanies behavior or policy changes. Transformation would be identified after project delivery as an impact of the efforts.)	*Objective 5.* Partners prepare programmatic, political, financial, and educational conditions for sustaining valuable student experiences derived from the project.
Objective 3. Include student perspectives and insights from the HCD process to help partners create a more valuable student experience.	*Objective 6.* Partners have such an exemplary innovation that it warrants consideration for scaling up or scaling out (this may require a time delay to measure).

ners have to anticipate the milestones on the path toward success and what the eventual goals might look like. This means that the key and challenging question is something like, "What gets measured in the face of a new problem?" Here, we use a set of process-based objectives (table 5.2), which, when implemented fully, link the success of the Hub, in aggregate, to the success of each project. Without an external standard, however, participation, iteration, and communication are essential in our project and partnership model.

Project-level objectives are typically co-developed in a project charter and can be assessed and researched at the end of the project, yielding information about the ways a project might move beyond outputs (e.g., a curriculum plan) to outcomes (the plan is adopted and implemented by faculty) to actual impact (students demonstrate more usable knowledge than previous comparable cohorts). Surveys, case studies, interviews, focus groups, program evaluations, and other more summative approaches are the typical methodologies used to gather information on the success of a project. Measures of student learning and progress toward degree completion can also be employed to help evaluate project goals. Assessing project objectives is a way to determine if and how the partner experienced actual changes as articulated in the project charter.

Organizational Uses of Assessment and Research

Once again, there is no design without assessment and research. While that has been true across our project portfolio, a statement like this means something different in higher education. We label forms of inquiry as *assessment* and *research* that might not be widely accepted inside higher education but that would be uncontroversial in other professional contexts. Our goal here is to provide case examples of assessment and research that have helped our design work succeed. Drawing from some of the longer-term projects in our portfolio, we intend to show how we have used more formal assessment and research in support of designing for change.

One of the more stable areas of work for the Hub has been in learning analytics,[11] which has taken various forms over the last several years. Initially, the desire for developing MSU's learning analytics function came from a general recognition that we needed to make better use of the data on campus to improve the institution, to leverage analytics in academic business processes, and to enhance students' ability to successfully complete their degrees. As is often the case at a large institution, small, decentralized (and loosely coupled) pockets of people all across campus were doing this work, but they lacked a coordinating body and the benefit of collaboration and knowledge-sharing. Moreover, for some functions we were relying on external vendors, who in the short term were useful to business practices but would eventually fail to meet the institution's needs. These vendor tools are generally designed for narrow-use cases and include proprietary models, which limits our ability to effectively use and adapt them.

In this milieu, MSU's Learning Analytics Group (LAG) was composed of individuals drawn from relevant units across campus and charged with the mission to coordinate and develop analytics resources and activities on campus (it was a good example of an "adhocracy," which we discuss in chapter 6). One goal of the group was to encourage a culture of data-driven decision-making in support of increasing the diversity and success of our students.

Encompassing the expertise of IT, administrative, curricular, and research professionals across campus, LAG existed to build and link together databases, analytical tools, and expertise for analyzing MSU's institutional data. The tool-building work enabled MSU to pursue policy-relevant research in order to effect specific improvements in undergraduate student learning and success at MSU, by means of course reform, curricular innovation, and advising practices. LAG was open to faculty and staff interested in using data to improve student learning and success, and most members worked with quantitative institutional data (data stored in university systems), classroom-level data, or both. The group intentionally drew participants from different units across campus, such as the Hub, IT, institutional research, undergraduate education, financial aid, and colleges and departments.

LAG became a group that encouraged data-informed leadership of the university with members collaborating across units, learning from other perspectives, discussing data issues and interpretation, and getting feedback for projects through friendly-yet-serious peer review. Within LAG, assessment work for the overall purpose of improving the student experience included projects such as investigating the effects of a cohort-based experience for first-year students in general studies courses; identifying admittance patterns and six-year outcomes for students with limited-enrollment majors (e.g., business and engineering); and assessing the likelihood for a student to go on probationary status, based on the probationary status of the roommates and floor mates within the university housing system, among many other factors.

One key example of LAG's success in this assessment work was the analytical work done to support MSU's credit momentum campaign. Administrators noticed an overall decrease in credit taking for the student body and a sharper decrease among students for whom we observed opportunity gaps (e.g., first-generation students). We also had indicators that those students who completed at least thirty credits in their first year maintained academic momentum and had better graduation outcomes. The indicators suggested that this was true across demographic categories and not simply the result of better-prepared and better-supported students taking more credits.

What followed was LAG's systematic analysis of our historical data to see, if it was true, what level of credit completion in the first year appeared to be related to good outcomes and to whom this applied. We learned enough to be comfortable with designing and pushing a credit-momentum campaign. The assessment of the campaign is ongoing, but it has been largely successful to date, increasing the number of students who are on track to complete their undergraduate degree in four years. Beyond the success of the program and the students themselves, the process itself was successful. As a coordinated system-wide effort to prioritize credit momentum, the process of changing rules, practices, and norms helped many individuals think differently about the idea of pushing (some) students to take additional credits. This and other LAG projects have addressed the overall design question of how to improve student success and close opportunity gaps at MSU. In acting on the analyses and reports, these activities were able to facilitate improving the student experience.

When it comes to research, we have developed a core set of staff, including graduate students interested in pursuing research projects within the portfolio, in addition to their own independent projects. Such work has included supporting and conducting design-based and other "translational" research focused on the student experience and student learning. When projects generated lessons that were surprising or generalizable enough to be valuable to a research literature and external colleagues, the project partners and Hub staff would report these impacts in conference papers and presentations as well as journal articles.

An important relationship in the Hub's portfolio that was fruitful for generating research products was a partnership between the Hub, the Department of Mathematics, the Program in Mathematics Education, and the Office of the Associate Provost for Undergraduate Education. In this work, staff in the Hub and the other partner units supported faculty in the Department of Mathematics as they made significant structural and curricular changes to introductory mathematics courses.

Specifically, a developmental course that, on the whole, was not supporting student success was replaced with a series of credit-bearing courses with embedded support to best facilitate success for students who placed at this level. Similar developmental (sometimes called remedial) mathematics courses are common across the landscape of higher education.[12] While the success rate for MSU students in this developmental course was reasonable in light of the large number of students nationally in developmental mathematics courses, faculty, staff, and students at MSU felt that students could be much better supported and, overall, more successful.

A major goal of the revised curricular pathways is to better prepare students with the mathematics that would be useful to them in their degree programs and future careers. Toward this end, students not tracking for calculus (e.g., those majoring in history) were able to fulfill the university mathematics graduation requirement by taking two newly developed quantitative literacy courses that explore the mathematics relevant to health and risk decisions, politics, finance, environmental issues, and other topics relevant to the students themselves.[13] These courses were designed with sufficient adaptive support that students who otherwise would have enrolled in the developmental algebra course could enroll directly in the quantitative literacy courses and still be successful at MSU.

Students who placed at the developmental level and had an interest in degree programs that require calculus (e.g., engineering) also had a new curricular path. Previously, these students would have taken one semester of developmental algebra and one semester of college-level algebra. In the revised pathway, some students now directly enroll in the college-level course while others take a two-semester "stretched" version of the college-level algebra course. While this new sequence still takes two semesters to finish, there are several added benefits: both college-level courses are credit-bearing, whereas the developmental course was not; the college-level courses are offered in relatively small, in-person course sections, whereas the developmental course was generally offered as one large, asynchronous online course; and the curriculum for the entire two-semester sequence is better aligned internally as well as streamlined for the follow-on calculus courses.

In evaluating the impact of these major curricular and structural changes, we assessed some aspects of the changes that were locally important (such as if and how the "backlog" of students needing to finish their university mathematics requirement were able to do so with the quantitative literacy courses). We also investigated several questions that we knew would be of wider interest, given that, at MSU and elsewhere, supporting students in introductory undergraduate mathematics courses is of paramount importance to those concerned with student success in STEM degree programs.[14]

Asking and answering these design questions through a research lens allowed us to identify the reasoning patterns students were using in one of the new quantitative literacy courses, explore the alignment between learning objectives and course assessments in the same quantitative literacy course, and quantitatively evaluate the effect of embedded remediation as a pathway for equitable access to introductory math courses.[15] These findings spurred conversations among scholars both within and outside the institution, and importantly, informed the design process.

Concluding Thoughts: Ethical Assessment and Research in a Third Space

In the midst of planning and carrying out these projects, we have gleaned some useful ideas for doing ethical assessment and research specifically in an organization like the Hub. There is no need here to reproduce a list of typical ethical considerations in scholarly work— taking care not to plagiarize sources, being transparent with the solicitation and inclusion of coauthors on reports and research products, facilitating a culture of informed consent, storing identified data securely, and so on. Such considerations are available in fine form elsewhere.[16] Here, instead, we share four considerations for doing ethical research and assessment work specifically in design organizations that are, perhaps, less obvious. We contend that these considerations emphasize an organizational culture of character, not personality.[17]

First, the pervasiveness of a busy culture in both higher education and American life more generally can lead to a frenetic pace of work, which is actually a liability. In many ways, students are subjected to the social norm that stuffing their schedules full of extra courses, work experiences, extracurricular clubs, and incessant volunteering are the keys to success following graduation. Faculty similarly commit to ancillary involvement in too many research projects, mentor groups that are too large, and agree to serve on too many committees. Whether real or perceived, the sense of busyness is palpable and feels increasingly acute with the fallout from the COVID-19 pandemic.

In this context, it is tempting for the assessment and research work in a design organization to follow a sense of commitment to everything and attempt to keep up with the "sprint" schedule in innovation. Such fast movement is not always productive toward the change goal. While design sprints are hugely important to projects, it is not sustainable or necessary for all projects to sprint. The pace of teaching and learning on which much of the Hub's research and assessment portfolio is built is slower than much of the other work we do in the Hub. Assessment projects, research projects, and indeed, change projects themselves, must be carried out with a laser-like focus and only sometimes with sprints, to deliver the product or process that will improve the partners' experience.

Second, the university is not nimble by default or design. In this slowly changing environment, it is important to think about moving fast and prototyping quickly, but we should not move fast simply for the sake of moving fast or because this helps us feel as if we are enacting change when we really are creating noise and burden. That is, some projects and indeed some changes require sustained attention, resources, and relationships that last for years. As Diane Sawyer has said, there is no substitute for paying attention, and some changes we seek might be measured—designed, even—in careers, not sprints.[18]

As an example, when we stewarded the design and creation of a new cocurricular record, scholar-practitioner staff conducted both research and assessment to create good designs for the record and also repeatable, theory-driven practices. In delivering the project, a new director of the project assumed ownership of the platform and began to develop practices to make it work in the long run. What was designed in the Hub will change the way students report on and value cocurricular experiences, but those designs were developed fairly quickly and then deliberately carried forward in a sustainable way within the context of the slowly changing university.

Third, it is important that a design organization intentionally make space for dissenting voices. Any organization on the edges of a traditional institution will draw some fire for being different. In our higher education context, we must be flexible enough to fully consider criticism of our assessment and research practices and honestly sort the beneficial from the rest. We ask ourselves which assessment and research practices are sacrosanct and valuable, and which are just sacrosanct. Organizations on the edges must be able to respect and learn from the systems from which they were born and indeed are trying to change. There is no room for an "us versus them" mentality, and myopic generalizations about the partners (generally faculty) are not helpful. In this way, those doing assessment and research in organizations like the Hub—and, indeed, the organization itself—requires a disposition of "generous orthodoxy," to borrow from theologian Hans Frei.[19] Change is hard for most people and organizations, and in our context, the Hub represents that change, quite noticeably. Holding open space to engage in dissent, as a means of creating understanding, is an important strategy for building trust and coalitions across the campus.

Fourth, change is both a short- and a long-term goal. Particularly for long-term change goals, research and assessment can yield good outcomes by supporting follow-through in the design work. After the reports are written and the papers published, much is revealed in the maintenance activities, or lack thereof, of those who completed the assessment or research, those who perhaps designed the broader project, and campus partners. That is, if assessment and research are foundational to a given design, we should look for and perhaps find some evidence of improved outcomes. A key component of designing for sustainability, then, is building in regular assessments and iterative improvements, even after the official "end" of the project; maintenance for the change, in other words. Depending on the nature of the project, someone involved from the design organization might conduct these follow-up assessment and research activities, but more likely someone in the local context would continue to follow the outcomes and identify evidence of change for the local community. Pushing for initial outcomes only at the surface level yields a performative, surface-level result in the long term.[20]

Finally, returning to the idea of the Hub as a "third space" organization, it is important to consider how credit is ascribed. On the whole, partnering units should be recognized as primary drivers and receive primary credit even when the balance of work falls to Hub staff. While this may seem unnecessary at best or disingenuous at worst, this disposition reflects that the Hub (unlike a traditional department) doesn't exist without partners to serve. In tension with the Hub's commitment to our partners' success is the Hub's willingness to be wrong. Given the possible constraints of busyness, pacing, and dissent, typical partners come to us seeking help because they believe the Hub will help them change efficiently. The paradox of efficient design, though, is taking small bets, missing a few (being wrong), and quickly improving. Communication of these expectations and paradigms is important for the Hub to be able to also absorb responsibility—to a point— for a change process not succeeding. Our successes only go as far as the successes of our partners, and in this way, the Hub exists as an organization supporting the work of the institution.

These ethical considerations, loaded as they are with complex power relationships, cannot be dismissed. They are integral to what it means to work in a loosely coupled system like MSU. It is true that assessment and research are typical activities in any institution of higher education, but conducting these activities in a design organization like the Hub requires particular kinds of attention. We don't practice within a department or enjoy the "protections" of disciplinarity. The campus community at large is generally unfamiliar with the role of research in design, and our efforts are, by definition, transdisciplinary and therefore require care, communication, and generosity.

At the same time, of course, the work can yield unforeseen collaborations and the opportunity for addressing new kinds of research questions. In addition to producing actual data and evidence that support decision-making around improving the student experience, doing research and assessment work confers some legitimacy to the organization since it mimics work that those in higher education are already familiar with. In this way, the assessment and research activities in the Hub have supported the overall success of the organization. More importantly, a commitment to research, assessment, and other forms of inquiry are required if we are designing.

6

Designing Requires a Design Organization

WHEN MICHIGAN STATE UNIVERSITY made the decision to move to remote teaching and work in early March of 2020, the campus was given two days to make the shift. Just six days earlier, a small team of Hub staff huddled around whiteboards to sketch how the university might approach a quick pivot to remote instruction. Administrators thought we might have ten days to figure this out, which we experienced as "unreasonable." So the virus gave us six.

MSU made an effective pivot to remote work, teaching, and learning, and we did so only because everyone on campus responded well to the challenge. Our ability to support faculty and students was a function of educators and professional development experts from across campus forming one team to respond. Yet it was the Hub that designed the response, and it was the culture of the Hub that sustained the response. In many respects, this chapter is about why that was the case. The first design project of the Hub was—and in some respects, still is—the Hub. This was true because we needed to build a new organization as we engaged in our work. Beyond that, however, we also needed to build a design operation. This chapter is about DesignOps and their importance for an effective design organization.

There is no design in higher education without a design organization.

In hindsight, March 2020 was a positive moment. The space of the Hub was transformed into the workspace for the teaching and learning pivot. It was from this space and team that next steps, decisions, work, and recommendations for campus emerged. MSU needed to design, and fast. We utilized our flexible and rapid processes as well as our facilitation practices. There was no time to fall into incremental change. No time for endless committees and meetings. No time for three-year cycles. No time for teaching and learning solutions disconnected from students' needs. No time for departmental silos that kept teams from collaborating. No time for questioning the value of design when it was delivering solutions at that very moment. We needed to sprint.

The Hub was effective in facilitating this work because we had built a strong team culture around ideas of design and processes to support them. Furthermore, that culture was shared or familiar to others: people were accustomed to working with the patterns we leveraged, working collaboratively, and creating conversations for solving problems. Our rhythms, pace, and practices worked because of the way the larger team worked. Culture and people pulled us through this moment, and because of that, we saw at scale how valuable design and a design organization can be in responding to the needs of higher education.

We had to change our work, too. Since March of 2020, the core Hub team rapidly moved design practices and collaborations into digital spaces, leveraging much of what we had already practiced with the support of a suite of digital collaboration tools. Project boards were now primarily located in the management tool Asana. Face-to-face meetings became Zoom video conferencing sessions. Whiteboard sessions became online whiteboard sessions on Mural. And sprints and workshops utilized all of these tools and spaces. In these ways, we continued to design ourselves and the way we work with the rest of the university amidst one of the biggest challenges higher education has faced in recent years. As we transitioned our work from spring and summer to fall and winter 2020, the team reflected on the Hub's efforts to continue iterating on our processes in digital spaces. We were reminded, once again, that whether online, face to face, or hybrid, we remained committed to helping the campus design transformative and equitable learning experiences. This same commitment has been central to the design of our own organization.

In the Beginning, an "All-Edge Adhocracy"

In order to support and nudge the university toward transformation, we began with ourselves, including important questions about what sort of design practice we needed to build. Questions of identity have been at the heart of our own process of discovery, and so for us to be able to design for higher education, we needed to create ourselves. We began, therefore, as something assembled at the edges of more stable organizations and functions inside MSU. We began as what Clay Spinuzzi calls an "all-edge adhocracy." All-edge adhocracies "temporarily [connect] specialists across organizations rather than just within organizations. They form briefly around a defined project, swarming it, then dispersing once it's completed. They change composition. They communicate, coordinate, and collaborate constantly, usually through digital information technologies. And they bring a level of flexibility, agility, and innovation that is unmatched by institutional hierarchies."[1]

All-edge adhocracies resist the commonplace practices of bureaucracies. As Spinuzzi reminds us, bureaucracy literally means "rule by desks or offices," and "rules" of this nature have been part and parcel to making "the members of an institutional hierarchy communicate, coordinate and cooperate efficiently." Bureaucracies can work well to simplify and speed things up, but organizational form and function by way of bureaucracy creates limitations: "By separating specialties, bureaucracies limit innovations that could come from crossing silos. By rewarding workers for following commands, bureaucracies tended to promote rule followers rather than innovators, reinforcing silos and resulting in managers who focused on guarding their turf . . . Moreover, bureaucracy proved unequal to so-called 'wicked problems.'"[2]

As we have discussed throughout this book, higher education faces a number of wicked problems, and we have certainly fancied ourselves as built to address them. Our own initial organization and way of working aligns with Spinuzzi's notion of an adhocracy. As he describes them, all-edge adhocracies are "interorganizational by nature," creating temporary organizations around projects, "interdisciplinary by necessity," needing multiple areas of expertise and viewpoints to address project challenges, and formed through "alliances" in which people jump in of their own volition and interest, serving both their and others' needs to address problems.[3] In our earliest organizational form, we certainly were more ad hoc than organized, and our way of operating in the present still functions very much as an adhocracy, in spirit if not in fact. This is fully consistent with our theory of institutional change (see introduction). We believe that change is most likely in those "zones of ambiguity." We seek those zones in our analytical work. We try to create them in our projects. The Hub itself is just that sort of zone of ambiguity.

It has been useful to us to explore how we fit the adhocracy mold. We can start with the fact that the Hub is focused on redesign through temporary projects at the edges of disciplines, units, and other functions. We work within and around the hierarchy of the university. At times we need those functional silos, because we pull individuals from units based on project need and attach them to a "temporary organization." We call that temporary organization a project. By way of projects, we cut across the organization, leveraging the capacity of structure to enable our function. Indeed, much of our work involves an orchestrated and temporary swarming of interdisciplinary expertise to address project challenges and opportunities and may involve people across and outside MSU. Innovation work in higher education is likely impossible without organizing people differently. By creating the Hub to function as an all-edge design adhocracy, we have been able to be nimbler and create different ways of working on problems together.

Adhocracy is one source of our effectiveness. Pulling people out of disciplinary and unit silos to leverage their expertise on problems that do not have disciplinary or organizational boundaries facilitates better problem-solving. In many ways, we still continue to function as an adhocracy, and we find ad hoc functions attractive. It is quietly transgressive in a way that suits us. Yet while this way of working is important, this way of organizing our work was not sustainable. To build more dynamic and sustainable academic design practices, which could also enable us to develop people, we needed to move beyond ad hoc. Many of the processes and patterns we developed are visible in earlier chapters. These patterns and processes are how we continue to grow our practice and our people. It quickly became clear, however, that for the Hub to be effective, we needed to build a design organization. Furthermore, it is now clear to us that to make change a part of the culture of higher education institutions, other colleges and universities will need a design organization as well. The next two sections, therefore, unpack how we built our design operations and professional development functions.

Design Ops

We have been inspired by thinking about the organization of design in industries outside higher education. According to its originator, Dave Malouf, DesignOps are "everything that supports high quality [design] crafts, methods, and processes."[4] In this context, operations "are the elements that facilitate high-quality instances of [design] activities with minimal friction" and include "the tools and infrastructure required to complete the [design] activity."[5] DesignOps are how a design organization organizes its design "tools, infrastructure, workflow, people, and governance" for smooth and optimal design outcomes, through a combined focus on design business operations, people operations, and workflow operations.[6]

An offshoot of Development Operations (DevOps), DesignOps has gained traction over the last five years as companies are scaling their design practices.[7] Because its main goal is to smooth out design processes for the design organization, it protects "the time and headspace of everyone within the design organization—the designers, writers, researchers, and so on—which allows everyone to focus on their respective craft."[8] At a certain moment in our development, it became clear that we needed to build our own DesignOps. People needed more structure, and our projects did, too. While our projects could continue to be experienced as an adhocracy relative to the larger university, the Hub could no longer function as an adhocracy.

DesignOps has risen in popularity as companies have needed more strategy concerning how to organize and leverage the value of design for their companies. As Merholz and Skinner paint the corporate design landscape, "most business leaders aren't designers, and so don't know how best to establish design in their organizations. Many design leaders with backgrounds in the practice of their craft, don't understand managerial and operational issues, and struggle with the organizational aspects of building and leading teams."[9] The Design Operations movement has been instrumental to our growth, providing guidance for how design can grow in an organization. We have, therefore, been able to leverage much of the learning, language, and patterns in the DesignOps community to guide us. DesignOps provide us with ideas for how to best structure our business, people, and workflow operations. The approach also provides key questions that any organization needs to ask and answer as it continues to mature: Who are we? What do we do? How do we communicate? What constrains us? How are we structured?[10] As we developed, we needed to answer these questions for ourselves. DesignOps was a key part of our identity work. It provided us with essential frames and questions through which we were able to articulate our values, our necessary infrastructure, and the processes that would best help us to realize them. This initial identity work led us to language and process that enabled tighter organization of our teams and our work. It also helped us to speak to internal and external audiences about the value of design. Imagine, for example, communicating our learning design process before we had settled on our own double diamond, and compare that to what became possible after we had settled on language and practices as represented in that process. It has been night and day with regard to our ability to communicate externally and develop individuals and teams internally. DesignOps was key to the identity work essential to building our shared design practices and then helping build our teams around those practices.

DesignOps has helped us to develop design teams in the Hub. We did this by paying attention to the skillsets we needed, learning to mix them on teams, providing teams with the support necessary, and moving toward an approximation of what Merholz and Skinner describe as a "centralized partnership."[11] The outcome was teams that combine learning experience design expertise with areas of expertise drawn from the learning sciences, educational technology, or educator professional development. Critical expertise, of course, is provided by our partners. We also supplement projects from domain expertise elsewhere on campus. One of the structural advantages of higher education is that our colleges and universities are expertise-rich, and our key stakeholders, students, are with us each day. Our emphasis has been on building strong design teams that have both design and subject matter expertise and are involved throughout all aspects of a project lifecycle.

Hiring and professional development have been part of our development of DesignOps as well (more on our professional development efforts below). The original Hub team was assembled by merging existing units on campus, supplemented by some focused hiring. We brought together individuals from information technology, instructional design, user experience, research, and teacher education to build our initial team. We knew we needed individuals who could work at the intersections of learning, experience design, and organizational change, and we knew our core team would need experience with change in educational organizations as well as institutional knowledge about the unique (and not so unique) aspects of working for a large research institution. This meant having people who knew how our university operates and how to best translate the academic practices they brought to our work to a range of oftentimes skeptical higher education audiences. It also meant gathering a team of individuals who could navigate the hierarchy of our higher ed institution while also executing in their specific areas of design expertise across both their team and other teams they might be collaborating with across campus.

Our teams use our double diamond as the foundation for our process (as outlined in chapter 2). We have also adapted agile work and project management practices to meet the needs of the design work we've described in this book. These agile work approaches include elements like standups, scrums, rapid prototyping, and regular iteration. They are also combined with the use of digital tools—for example, Slack, Microsoft Teams, Zoom, Google Docs, and Mural—to allow teams located across campus to easily collaborate and execute work both synchronously and asynchronously. In fact, we found that our agile practices and use of these tools were a key part of our success in recently moving to remote work. Our swift adaptability is a byproduct of our DesignOps and our continuous attentiveness to learning and growth.

Our central management operation has been designed to support a flat design operation. The core management team combines our director, associate director, project manager, head of communications, chief digital officer, and Hub staff, rotating monthly through team meetings. The central function of the management team has been to guide the strategy of the design organization, lead the project funnel, and support team professional development. As we have noted, in our attempt to continue to cultivate a flat culture, staff members, design brief authors, and subject matter experts from the rest of the team and beyond the Hub often join to contribute to decision-making for the organization. Our teams and our organization report up through our provost's office and are further supported by executive leadership across our university. Here again, by focusing on building a design operation, we built our organization in a manner that supported our mission and purpose.

We believe, as does DesignOps pioneer Dave Malouf, that the "mission for the practice of DesignOps [is to] amplify the value of design."[12] While the Hub has had strong executive support, we were left to our own devices to figure out how to execute. Our design operation empowers our learning experience designers to be involved in the full project cycle. They play a key role in problem-framing and guiding the direction of the team into prototyping and beyond. This flies in the face of what has been common not only in higher education but also in other design organizations. There, designers aren't as often engaged in the problem-framing, strategy, and inquiry related to a project, and instead are asked to simply execute what has already been decided.[13] Our approach allows for the project team to focus on the full cycle of design work and to place as much value on the design inquiry as on the project execution and production. Our collective approach to design has helped us to share a common language from framing to execution and to build a shared commitment to the value of design for education. This framework has also provided important language for articulating the practices we need to share at the core of our work, which has been crucial for us in designing ourselves to be the kind of design organization and university model we hope to be.

Learning to Be a Design Organization

Building a design organization is more than structure and process. We needed to learn to *be* a design organization. Therefore, much of our work to build a design organization has focused on learning. Our version of the double-diamond design process provided language and framing around design processes, but it was also not well understood or adopted by a new team. Therefore, we needed to live our own process and create divergent and convergent approaches to our own professional development as we built a design organization.

To align and navigate our common expertise and multidisciplinary approaches to design, professional development quickly became an integral part of our teamwork. We created a baseline understanding of these different areas of professional development by creating a common professional development experience for our team. Over time, we have continued to adapt our professional development each time our team grew or evolved, or as our processes changed to adapt to the needs of projects.

Our professional development matches the trajectory of our design process. We created a sequence focused on *Discovery*, which entails adapting research practices to the sorts of inquiry we were seeing in our project portfolio. This sequence is in many ways an exploration of research methods common to learning design practices, braided with insights from discipline-based research practices. If our job is to facilitate and support teams engaged in discovery work, then we need to grow our collective and individual ability to participate in that work. We continue with a related sequence of activities concerned with *Define*. Here our efforts are even more intentionally focused on user needs and requirements and how to use data analysis, for example, as a bridge from discovery to definition. Our focus on these moments in the design process is deeper, for two reasons. We learned as a team that this was the primary area of need, and we learned from our project work that strong facilitation of the discovery phase is required to prevent the equally strong impulses of project teams to close projects too soon by arriving at solutions too quickly.

Perhaps the best way to illustrate the importance of learning to the building of our design organization is through an extended example of an extended professional development process designed to encompass the entirety of our design process. We wanted this moment to be embodied, proximal, and prolonged for a few reasons. First, we know from cognitive approaches to learning that we learn by constructing knowledge or meaning-making through experience, so we wanted our professional development to be applied and not solely theoretical.[14] Second, we needed to use a project that was both familiar to the team, yet low-stakes enough to live in what Vygotsky called the zone of proximal development, that distance between what a learner can do without help and what they can do with support from someone with more knowledge or expertise.[15] And third, a prolonged approach allowed for a version of a "spiral curriculum" as an iterative revisiting and deepening of topics through time.[16] We referred to that professional development experience as the Hub main street experience redesign.

Over the years, the Hub physical space had been the subject of as many design iterations as the Hub team itself. One area of the space that serves many purposes is "main street," a strip of open space where we display our project boards. But main street is literally the main street through the space, enabling access to all of the other functional areas of the Hub (conference room, focus rooms, staff break room, open workshop area, and staff work area.) The most important use of main street is as the location for our Monday morning stand-up meeting, a reporting moment that sets the scene for our work. The purpose of stand-up is for the team, but the meeting itself is open, and we nearly always have guests. Guests come because they are associated with a project being reported, or they are curious about our portfolio or processes. Therefore, our reporting has a built-in audience problem. The team was interested in solving the problem. Furthermore, while functional, the main street space itself is not necessarily inviting or conducive to our values: an open, welcoming space that encourages potential partners and guests to collaborate. So, we decided to use the activity of reporting on main street as our common professional development opportunity: How might we redesign the main street experience?

Main Street Experience Redesign

The guiding prompt for this professional development experience was:

> Hub management would like help in redesigning the Hub main street experience. The Hub main street functions as both a front door to the Hub for project partners and visitors, sharing the latest in Hub projects, as well as a weekly gathering place for the Hub's stand-up and project reporting. As the Hub will be moving all its projects into a new project management tool and eventually moving into a new physical space in 2020, the main street experience will be changing. Additionally, staff, management, and outside partners have, at points, shared confusion about the overall function of main street, finding it difficult to understand key information, share and receive feedback about project designs, and even feeling that main street sometimes communicates disorganization(s). With the shift in project management tools and a move in the

near future, now is a perfect time to reimagine the Hub main street experience.

Three small teams of four or five individuals were formed for the duration of the six-week professional development (PD) experiences. Each team focused on different aspects of the main street experience:

- How might we arrange objects in the Hub to give partners, employees, and visitors a sense of welcome, making them feel inspired to design learning experiences with us?
- How might we create a reporting experience that meets organizational purposes but is creative, fun, and engaging?
- How might we welcome new visitors to the space so that they feel welcomed and are clear about how to engage with the space?

It is important to be clear that we are not architects or space designers. The point of the experience was not to leverage expertise we don't have. The point was to practice design. Therefore, we emphasized the importance of dedicating time to design inquiry and problem-framing in order to better understand the problem or opportunity and the needs of our partners on any given project. As Merholz and Skinner explain, "problem solving is only the tip of the iceberg for design. Beneath the surface, design is a powerful tool for problem framing, ensuring that what is being addressed is worth tackling. Go deeper still, and you discover that the core opportunity for design is to inject humanism into work."[17] For that purpose, each team conducted interviews with Hub project partners, newcomers, and regular visitors to gather information about their lived experiences of the space. Teams also conducted observations of the space at different times of the day. The goal was to further familiarize the team with shared inquiry and research methodologies. We also encouraged teams to look at analogous examples from other spaces and industries that were looking at solving similar challenges. This allowed the teams to gain inspiration and be creative in their problem-framing before prototyping different solutions.

Prototypes consisted of

- a set of signage upon entry to the Hub space (chalk drawings, arrows, name plates, ceiling signs); a front-desk kiosk; a creative play station (mini hockey in open space); a creative space with books, coffee table and chairs, puzzles, design quotes, etc.;
- trying out narrative-driven styles of reporting during stand-up; changing project board design; streamlining project boards structure across projects; and
- a reception desk with a greeter; propping open the door; displaying a map of the space at the entrance; writing out the meetings for the day.

Teams constructed these prototypes and tested them with a range of users before producing an insight report as the main deliverable of the experience. Insights included items such as:

- People interpret and use Hub space in different ways; users of the space appreciate clear directions; prototyping culture is learned and cultivated internally first, before being shared with partners; prototyping is a continuous activity (not a one-shot practice).
- Organizing project boards by categories creates more narrative flow for reporting; storytelling around the project helps people understand how to understand and engage with them; location of boards gives an opportunity to group projects strategically.
- Signs and directions help: people appreciate knowing the name of the meeting and the name of the person who booked the meeting, and maps direct visitors to rooms that aren't visible when visitors first enter the space.

Finally, teams were asked to provide some recommendations based on their work:

- Embed creativity in the space; showcase prototyping as a regular activity; familiarize the whole staff with prototyping and creativity practices; use signage and wayfinding objects to orient and identify important spaces in our workspace.

- Providing guidance on how to navigate our space helps our visitors to feel as if they belong.
- Reorganize all project boards based on four key work areas: design, research, digital strategy, and digital collaboration; share narrative reporting prompts and recruit other projects to adopt; continue to test and gather and share experiences of implementation.
- Incorporate a permanent map into the welcome area for visitors to orient themselves to the space; have a reception desk with a greeter.

The fact that the professional development experience lasted six weeks, involved the whole team, and was visible in our space had lasting effects on our operation. The experience may have been most valuable as a team-building activity, which helped us to discover talents and expertise that had not surfaced before. For instance, one staff member used his user experience and technical skills to create digital signage as part of a prototype; some individuals explored creative ways to think about gamifying reporting procedures; and others discovered ingenious ways to conduct interviews and observations. More importantly, we used professional development the same way we use conversation design around learning experiences: to build relationships and encourage change as a mindset. Indeed, becoming a unified team around Hub processes, language, and practices created affordances for team bonding and more substantial professional relationships. Foundational to building the organization has been building the relationships between and among people. "Getting people right" includes getting our own people right.

Over time, we built what we call "patterns," or repeatable examples of how we have facilitated conversations across the phases of our design process. Those patterns eventually made it possible to imagine our own learning experience design (LXD) playbook. Company playbooks are common in many industries. They merge the essence of athletic team playbooks, which contain strategies and plays, with the original intent of Elizabethan drama playbooks, which provided actors with stage directions. Our playbook is a repository of strategies and information about learning theories, design thinking activities, relationship-building strategies, and project management for change in higher education. We built the playbook as a collective way to solidify our approach to LXD while expanding our shared understanding of how to execute LXD projects. The playbook is very much the story of our DesignOps, and more importantly, the story of the people who have come together to build it.

As we continue with our use of professional development to build DesignOps, we are paying attention to what we need as an organization to continue to grow and mature. We are extending our learning practices into how we hire and retain talent. As we do so, we are asking

- what key design skills can help push our design organization forward?
- what professional paths are associated with our approach to LXD? and
- how might we best support the growth of our learning experience designers?

We also continue to learn what our team needs to be, do, and know to be successful, such as

- working dynamically at the edge of disciplines and university structures;
- combining expertise in multiple learning experience design areas;
- sharing a common set of design processes and iterating on design practices;
- leveraging collaboration tools (analog and digital) to support dynamic teaming practices;
- committing to learning as a core job expectation; and
- supporting professional development to realize career trajectories.

Our team has grown individually by way of our commitment to shared learning. That individual growth is a function of operational maturity. A shared organizational commitment to learning has been the primary pathway for building a design organization.

Sprinting into the Future: Design Forward

We are an internal design consultancy for MSU. We focus on designing transformative learning experiences. We leverage design because of its affordances in imagining and making new relationships in higher education. We leverage what Malouf calls "deconstructive creativity," or envisioning "a rough idea of a whole system, only to tear it apart and rebuild it."[18] Deconstructive creativity is a byproduct of what Malouf has also called "serendipity by design," a key part of a design studio culture, which regularly creates collisions between ideas and people.[19] The importance of building a design operation and learning to think and act like a design organization is that it enables a productive studio culture. That culture holds shared practices, and those practices, in turn, facilitate working with project partners on the challenges they bring to us and the joyful effort to deconstruct, redesign, and reconstruct new possibilities for ourselves and our institution.

Our own design operations are extremely helpful for articulating design for our colleagues in a way we can all understand and practice. Our approach also allows for variation to take on a range of projects beyond curriculum or course design. Ultimately, we hope the value we provide is more transformative and equitable learning experiences at the level of the course, program, or institution. The Hub still has a way to go in our larger project of becoming our university's design organization. We have, however, moved beyond being a "startup" because of our work on design operations. We have used the frameworks shared in this chapter and across the book to establish processes, shared language, and an emerging track record of project impact. They have been essential to establishing our design organization.

The design organization necessary to facilitate change in higher education must build and hold the institution's design culture. That design organization supports designers and speaks to the value of design for the institution. It also finds ways to communicate the impact of design and provides opportunities for executive stakeholders across the university to experience the value that design can bring. Via its learning function, the design organization shares emerging practices and enables organizational development. In these ways, the design organization helps to cultivate a design culture across the institution. Others in higher education who wish to walk this path with us will have to ask and answer many of the same questions we've asked in this chapter: What ongoing skills will be needed in order to reach the necessary level of design maturity for impact? What is required to develop, learn, and build culture? How do we execute? We hope this book, but particularly this chapter on design operations, provides a head start.

As we close, we note that we continue to design in response to the ongoing pandemic. We have supported key projects related to student experience and to ongoing educator professional development. We are seeing growing interest in "sprinting" as a way of working. Recently, for example, we facilitated a design sprint focused on how students could return to campus for the Spring 2021 semester. This exercise was focused on student success outcomes, namely, which students need to learn on campus in order to persist and graduate and which students need to live on campus to achieve the same outcomes. Prior "reopening" efforts had taken months, involved many committees, accomplished a great deal, but left us facing a spring without the level of specificity required to "open" the campus more fully to students. We built on that effort but focused on what learning experiences were required to best support students safely coming back to campus.

For this sprint, we gathered individuals in teams representing areas with relevant domain expertise. Much of our focus was on figuring out not only which students needed to live or learn on campus but also what support was necessary to make that return safe and impactful. Team members worked through Zoom and Mural across a facilitated design process to investigate these areas. Across the first couple of sprint days, some people expressed skepticism about the extent to which the process would produce the necessary results. Others also quickly jumped to solutions. They also expressed appreciation for being invited into the work, excitement about engaging with colleagues they wouldn't normally work with, and hope for what might be done in our short time together. The teams started with better questions than they might have otherwise come up with in their functional silos and created useful ways to map the problem space they tackled. They asked and answered—quickly—basic, essential, important questions and ultimately designed solutions that constituted a set of recommendations to the president and the provost. The goal was to give executives a decision-making matrix with a focus on what was most needed for our students at that very time. These solutions guided the decisions of the university at a crucial moment. As we argue in this book, it's these moments that underline the power of design to help us understand problems and create opportunities.

Throughout this book, we have argued that design must become a core competency of the university, and we leveraged design cases to make arguments about how to facilitate change in higher education. More importantly, we argued that to do this work requires a design organization. In a series of three chapters, we focused on learning experience design as an increasingly critical practice at the nexus of learning sciences, experience design, and change management. We then described our operationalization of LXD through design thinking, systems thinking, and futures thinking, as we incorporated a number of familiar design processes and patterns to remix them in ways uniquely suited to address the challenges of the higher educational context. We also developed our constructivist view of designing conversations and proposed that the way we design for conversations about learning experiences is crucial to encourage innovation in higher education. Design conversations are tools for change and position the learning experience designer as change facilitator.

In chapter 4, we put forward an understanding of change management as design: our projects are change management projects, but change management isn't a common approach in most academic settings. As the book concludes, we looked at the role of assessment and research in a design organization, including the assessment of innovative designs that inform decision-making to the production of scholarly work that contributes to a research domain. The journey ends with this sixth and final chapter, which deals with DesignOps and the need to build a design organization through principles and practices that have guided the design of the organization itself.

In this way, we've presented the work of the Hub for Innovation in Learning and Technology at Michigan State University as an argument. We can and should design the next iteration of higher education. To do so requires colleges and universities to build design functions as a core capacity. We hope our example is useful to our colleagues in higher education who share our path and who also must build, design, and support faculty, staff, and students to work toward a more equitable, sustainable, and transformative university experience.

NOTES

Introduction. *Designing Change in Higher Education*

1. Doug Lederman, "Not Future-Ready," *Inside Higher Education*, Oct. 22, 2019, https://www.insidehighered.com/digital-learning/article/2019/10/22/four-year -college-leaders-not-feeling-ready-future.

2. Cathy N. Davidson, *The New Education: How to Revolutionize the University to Prepare Students for a World in Flux* (New York: Basic Books, 2017), 248.

3. William Moner, Phillip Motley, and Rebecca Pope-Ruark, "Introduction: A Radical Vision for Redesigning Liberal Education," in *Redesigning Liberal Education: Innovative Design for a Twenty-First-Century Undergraduate Education*, ed. William Moner, Phillip Motley, and Rebecca Pope-Ruark (Baltimore: Johns Hopkins Univ. Press, 2020), 8. In that same collection, see also Randy Bass, "Can We Liberate Liberal Education?" This body of work is consistent with contextually responsive yet holistic treatments, such as those from Michael Roth, *Beyond the University: Why Liberal Education Matters* (New Haven, CT: Yale Univ. Press, 2014), and Chris Gallagher, *College Made Whole: Integrative Learning for a Divided World* (Baltimore: Johns Hopkins Univ. Press, 2019).

4. William G. Bowen and Michael S. McPherson, *Lesson Plan: An Agenda for Change in American Higher Education* (Princeton, NJ: Princeton Univ. Press, 2016).

5. Davidson, *The New Education*, 4.

6. David F. Labaree, *A Perfect Mess: The Unlikely Ascendancy of American Higher Education* (Chicago: Univ. of Chicago Press, 2017), 1, https://doi.org/10.7208 /chicago/9780226250588.001.0001.

7. Labaree, 23.

8. Labaree, 23.

9. Adrianna Kezar, *How Colleges Change: Understanding, Leading, and Enacting Change* (New York: Routledge, 2014), 3.

10. Labaree, *A Perfect Mess*, 248.

11. Joshua Kim and Edward Maloney, *Learning Innovation and the Future of Higher Education*, Tech.Edu: A Hopkins Series on Education and Technology (Baltimore: Johns Hopkins Univ. Press, 2020), 2–3.

12. Kim and Maloney, 4–5.

13. Kim and Maloney, 6.

14. Kim and Maloney, 5.

15. Davidson, *The New Education*, 248.

16. Kim and Maloney, *Learning Innovation and the Future of Higher Education*, 10.

17. Kim and Maloney, 7.

18. James E. Porter et al., "Institutional Critique: A Rhetorical Methodology for Change," *College Composition and Communication* 51, no. 4 (2000): 613, https://doi.org/10.2307/358914.

19. Porter et al., 625.

20. Porter et al., 611.

21. Ezio Manzini, *Design, When Everybody Designs: An Introduction to Design for Social Innovation* (Cambridge, MA: MIT Press, 2015), 1, https://doi.org/10.7551/mitpress/9873.001.0001.

22. Manzini, 1.

23. Richard Buchanan, "Rhetoric, Humanism, and Design," in *Discovering Design: Explorations in Design Studies*, ed. Richard Buchanan and Victor Margolin (Chicago: Univ. of Chicago Press, 1995), 25.

24. Paul Pangaro, "Cybernetics As Phoenix: Why Ashes, What New Life?," in *Cybernetics: State of the Art*, ed. Liss C. Werner, 2017, 23, https://doi.org/10.14279/DEPOSITONCE-6121.

25. Pangaro, 16.

26. Beronda Montgomery, "From Deficits to Possibilities: Mentoring Lessons from Plants on Cultivating Individual Growth through Environmental Assessment and Optimization," *Public Philosophy Journal* 1, no. 1 (2018): 1.

27. Steven Mintz, "Why We Need Centers for Educational Innovation, Evaluation, and Research," *Inside Higher Education*, Nov. 30, 2020, https://www.insidehighered.com/blogs/higher-ed-gamma/why-we-need-centers-educational-innovation-evaluation-and-research.

28. Rachel Cooper and Sabine Junginger, "General Introduction: Design Management—A Reflection," in *The Handbook of Design Management*, ed. Rachel Cooper, Sabine Junginger, and Thomas Lockwood (London: Bloomsbury, 2011), 23.

29. Angela Meyer, "Embedding Design Practice within Organizations," in Cooper, Junginger, and Lockwood, 188.

30. Meyer, 196.

31. Meyer, 188.

32. Meyer, 188.

33. Relative to most of US higher education, MSU does very well with its six-year graduation rate and extremely well relative to predictions for our graduation rate given the composition of our student body. This means that moving our overall rate even a few percentage points is difficult and expensive. But it also means that we cannot do it without erasing the opportunity gaps.

Chapter 1. Learning Experience Design in Higher Education

1. Martin Smith, "MIT Proposes New Role of "Learning Engineer," Jan. 10, 2017, https://www.capdm.com/index.php/2017/01/10/mit-proposes-new-role-of-learning-engineer/.

2. Karen Wilcox, Sanjay Sarma, and Philip Lippel, "Online Education: A Catalyst for Higher Education Reforms," 2016, 26, https://oepi.mit.edu/files/2016/09/MIT-Online-Education-Policy-Initiative-April-2016.pdf.

3. National Research Council, *Discipline-Based Education Research: Understanding and Improving Learning in Undergraduate Science and Engineering* (Washington, DC: National Academies Press, 2012), 9, https://doi.org/10.17226/13362.

4. Elaine Beirne and Matthew P. Romanoski, "Instructional Design in Higher Education: Defining an Evolving Field" (Online Learning Consortium, 2018), https://onlinelearningconsortium.org/read/instructional-design-in-higher-education-defining-an-evolving-field/; Joshua A. Kirby, Christopher M. Hoadley, and Alison A. Carr-Chellman, "Instructional Systems Design and the Learning Sciences: A Citation Analysis," *Educational Technology Research and Development* 53, no. 1 (2005): 37–47, https://doi.org/10.1007/BF02504856.

5. For a coherent book-length treatment, see Bruce M. Mackh, *Higher Education by Design: Best Practices for Curricular Planning and Instruction* (New York: Routledge, 2018).

6. Spiros Soulis, Angela Nicolettou, and Joyce Seitzinger, "Using Learner Experience Design (LX) for Program Enhancement" (Conference Expanding Horizons in Open & Distance Learning, Australia, 2017).

7. Whitney Kilgore, "UX to LX: The Rise of Learner Experience Design," *EdSurge* (blog), June 20, 2016, https://www.edsurge.com/news/2016-06-20-ux-to-lx-the-rise-of-learner-experience-design.

8. Soulis, Nicolettou, and Seitzinger, "Using Learner Experience Design (LX) for Program Enhancement," 3.

9. M. Brown et al., "2020 Educause Horizon Report Teaching and Learning Edition" (EDUCAUSE, 2020), 23, https://www.learntechlib.org/p/215670/.

10. James Dalziel et al., "The Larnaca Declaration on Learning Design—2013," in *Learning Design: Conceptualizing a Framework for Teaching and Learning Online*, ed. James Dalziel (New York: Routledge, 2016), 6.

11. Gráinne Conole, "Theoretical Underpinnings of Learning Design," in Daziel, *Learning Design*, 59.

12. Dalziel et al., "The Larnaca Declaration on Learning Design—2013," 16.

13. Eva Dobozy and Chris Campbell, "The Complementary Nature of Learning Design and TPACK," in Dalziel, *Learning Design*, 99.

14. Diana Laurillard, "Preface," in Dalziel, *Learning Design*, viii.

15. Brown et al., "2020 Educause Horizon Report Teaching and Learning Edition," 23.

16. Thomas Wendt, *Design for Dasein: Understanding the Design of Experiences* (Charleston, SC: Createspace, 2015), 12.

17. See Mary Helen Immordino-Yang and Antonio Damasio, "We Feel, Therefore We Learn: The Relevance of Affective and Social Neuroscience to Education," *Mind, Brain, and Education* 1, no. 1 (2007): 3–10, https://doi.org/10.1111/j.1751-228X.2007.00004.x.

18. Christian Madsbjerg and Mikkel B. Rasmussen, *The Moment of Clarity:*

Using the Human Sciences to Solve Your Toughest Business Problems (Boston: Harvard Business Review Press, 2014), 76–77.

19. Madsbjerg and Rasmussen, 78.

20. Christian Madsbjerg, *Sensemaking: The Power of the Humanities in the Age of the Algorithm* (New York: Hachette Books, 2017), 7.

21. Madsbjerg, 16.

22. Madsbjerg, 21.

23. Brown et al., "2020 Educause Horizon Report Teaching and Learning Edition," 24.

24. Joshua Kim and Edward Maloney, *Learning Innovation and the Future of Higher Education*, Tech.Edu: A Hopkins Series on Education and Technology (Baltimore: Johns Hopkins Univ. Press, 2020), 113.

25. Kim and Maloney, 122–23.

26. Brown et al., "2020 Educause Horizon Report Teaching and Learning Edition," 24.

27. David D. Dill, "The Regulation of Public Research Universities: Changes in Academic Competition and Implications for University Autonomy and Accountability," *Higher Education Policy*, 14, no. 1 (2001): 21–35; Ellen Hazelkorn, "Learning to Live with League Tables and Ranking: The Experience of Institutional Leaders," *Higher Education Policy*, 21, no. 2 (2008): 193–215; Peter D. Eckel and Adrianna Kezar. "Key Strategies for Making New Institutional Sense: Ingredients to Higher Education Transformation," *Higher Education Policy* 16, no. 1 (2003): 39–53.

28. Kim and Maloney, *Learning Innovation and the Future of Higher Education*, 126.

29. We can overvalue the idea that disciplinarity equals respect in higher education. It takes a great deal of humility for ranked faculty to value those who aren't also ranked faculty or from their discipline or field. That humility is in short supply at many institutions. Smith, "MIT Proposes New Role of 'Learning Engineer.'"

30. See their own discussion in this regard. Kim and Maloney, *Learning Innovation and the Future of Higher Education*, 132–39.

31. Kate Stohr and Cameron Sinclair; Architecture for Humanity, ed., *Design Like You Give a Damn [2]: Building Change from the Ground Up* (New York: Abrams, 2012).

32. Madsbjerg, *Sensemaking*, 192.

Chapter 2. Operationalizing Design

1. Yana Milev, "Outline of an Expanded Concept of Design in the Field of the (Empirical) Cultural Sciences," in *D.A: A Transdisciplinary Handbook of Design Anthropology*, ed. Yana Milev (Frankfurt am Main: Peter Lang, 2013), 18–39.

2. Hazel Clark and David Eric Brody, eds., "Introduction to Design Studies: A Reader," in *Design Studies: A Reader* (Oxford: Berg, 2009), 1.

3. Horst W. J. Rittel and Melvin M. Webber, "Dilemmas in a General Theory of Planning," *Policy Sciences* 4, no. 2 (1973): 155–69, https://doi.org/10.1007/BF01405730.

4. Jeffrey W. Lucas and Amy R. Baxter, "Power, Influence, and Diversity in Organizations," *Annals of the American Academy of Political and Social Science* 639, no. 1 (2012): 49–70.

5. S. Blank, "Why Companies Do 'Innovation Theater' Instead of Actual Innovation," *Harvard Business Review* (blog), Oct. 7, 2019, https://hbr.org/2019/10/why-companies-do-innovation-theater-instead-of-actual-innovation.

6. Thomas Wendt, *Design for Dasein: Understanding the Design of Experiences* (Charleston, SC: Createspace, 2015), 66.

7. Peter G. Rowe, *Design Thinking* (Cambridge, MA: MIT Press, 1987).

8. Stefanie Di Russo, "Understanding the Behaviour of Design Thinking in Complex Environments" (PhD thesis, Melbourne: Swinburne University, 2016), 11–21.

9. R. Conway, J. Masters, and J. Thorold, *From Design Thinking to Systems Change: How to Invest in Innovation for Social Impact* (London: Royal Society of Arts, Action and Research Centre, 2017).

10. Conway, Masters, and Thorold, 3.

11. Wendt, *Design for Dasein*, 150.

12. Peter M. Senge, *The Fifth Discipline: The Art and Practice of the Learning Organization*, rev. ed. (New York: Doubleday/Currency, 2006); Donella H. Meadows, *Thinking in Systems: A Primer* (White River Junction, VT: Chelsea Green, 2008).

13. Senge, *The Fifth Discipline*, 3.

14. Tatiana Fumasoli and Bjørn Stensaker, "Organizational Studies in Higher Education: A Reflection on Historical Themes and Prospective Trends," *Higher Education Policy* 26, no. 4 (2013): 479.

15. Anthony Dunne and Fiona Raby, *Speculative Everything: Design, Fiction, and Social Dreaming* (Cambridge, MA: MIT Press, 2013); Organisation for Economic Co-operation and Development OECD, "Futures Thinking," *Schooling for Tomorrow Knowledge Base* (blog), Feb. 26, 2016, https://www.oecd.org/site/schoolingfortomorrowknowledgebase/futuresthinking/; Rafael Ramírez, John W. Selsky, and Kees Van der Heijden, eds., *Business Planning for Turbulent Times: New Methods for Applying Scenarios*, Science in Society Series, 2nd ed. (London: Earthscan, 2010).

16. See Rafael Ramírez, Riku Österman, and Daniel Grönquist, "Scenarios and Early Warnings as Dynamic Capabilities to Frame Managerial Attention," *Technological Forecasting and Social Change* 80, no. 4 (2013): 825–38, https://doi.org/10.1016/j.techfore.2012.10.029; Sohail Inayatullah, "Six Pillars: Futures Thinking for Transforming," *Foresight* 10, no. 1 (22, 2008): 4–21, https://doi.org/10.1108/14636680810855991; D. H. Ingvar, "Memory of the Future: An Essay on the Temporal Organization of Conscious Awareness," *Human Neurobiology* 4, no. 3 (1985): 127–36.

17. René Rohrbeck and Hans Georg Gemünden, "Corporate Foresight: Its Three Roles in Enhancing the Innovation Capacity of a Firm," *Technological Forecasting and Social Change* 78, no. 2 (2011): 231–43, https://doi.org/10.1016/j.techfore.2010.06.019.

18. Patricia M. Shields and Nandhini Rangarajan, *A Playbook for Research*

Methods: Integrating Conceptual Frameworks and Project Management, New Forums Scholarly Writing Series (Stillwater, OK: New Forum Press, 2013).

19. Randall Teal, "Developing a (Non-Linear) Practice of Design Thinking," *International Journal of Art & Design Education* 29, no. 3 (2010): 295, https://doi.org /10.1111/j.1476-8070.2010.01663.x.

20. British Design Council, "Double Diamond Updated Framework," 2019, https://www.designcouncil.org.uk/news-opinion/what-framework-innovation -design-councils-evolved-double-diamond; IDEO, ed., *The Field Guide to Human-Centered Design: Design Kit* (San Francisco: IDEO, 2015); Stanford d.School, "Get Started with Design Thinking," *Stanford d.School* (blog), 2010, https://dschool .stanford.edu/resources/getting-started-with-design-thinking.

21. Sheri Tishman and Patricia Palmer, "Visible Thinking," *Leadership Compass* 2, no. 4 (2005): 1–3.

22. Icek Ajzen, "The Theory of Planned Behavior," *Organizational Behavior and Human Decision Processes* 50, no. 2 (1992): 179–211.

23. Wendt, *Design for Dasein*.

24. Wendt, 134.

25. Holger Steinmetz et al., "How Effective Are Behavior Change Interventions Based on the Theory of Planned Behavior? A Three-Level Meta-Analysis," *Zeitschrift für Psychologie* 224, no. 3 (2016): 216–33, https://doi.org/10.1027/2151 -2604/a000255.

26. Brené Brown, *Dare to Lead: Brave Work, Tough Conversations, Whole Hearts* (New York: Random House, 2018).

27. Brené Brown, "TED Talk: The Power of Vulnerability," https://www.ted .com/talks/brene_brown_the_power_of_vulnerability?language=en.

28. Tim Brown and Barry Katz, *Change by Design: How Design Thinking Transforms Organizations and Inspires Innovation* (New York: Harper Business, 2009), 132.

29. Brown and Katz, 132.

Chapter 3. Designing Conversations

1. Kurt Lewin, *Field Theory in Social Science; Selected Theoretical Papers* (New Delhi: Isha Books, 2013).

2. See Kathleen Manning, *Organizational Theory in Higher Education* (New York: Routledge, 2017).

3. Louise Morley, "Does Class Still Matter? Conversations about Power, Privilege and Persistent Inequalities in Higher Education," *Discourse: Studies in the Cultural Politics of Education* 41, no. 1 (2020): 1–12.

4. Morley, 1.

5. Tom Delph-Janiurek, "'Walking the Walk and Talking the Talk': Bodies, Conversation, Gender and Power in Higher Education in England," *Social & Cultural Geography* 1, no. 1 (2000): 83–100.

6. Phil S. Ensor, "The Functional Silo Syndrome" (*AME Target*, Spring 1988).

7. David Bohm, Donald Factor, and Peter Garrett, "Dialogue—A Proposal," 1991, http://www.david-bohm.net/dialogue/dialogue_proposal.html, 3.

8. Paul Pangaro, "Designing Conversations for Socially-Conscious Design" (RSD5 Conference, Ontario College of Art & Design, Toronto, Canada, 2016), https://www.pangaro.com/rsd5/index.html.

9. Vera John-Steiner and Teresa Meehan, "Creativity and Collaboration in Knowledge Construction," in *Vygotskian Perspectives on Literacy Research: Constructing Meaning through Collaborative Inquiry*, ed. Carol D. Lee and Peter Smagorinsky (Cambridge: Cambridge Univ. Press, 2000), 31–51.

10. Gordon Pask, *Conversation, Cognition, and Learning* (New York: Elsevier, 1975); Jack Sidnell and Tanya Stivers, eds., *The Handbook of Conversation Analysis: Sidnell/The Handbook of Conversation Analysis* (Chichester, UK: John Wiley & Sons, 2012), https://doi.org/10.1002/9781118325001.

11. Hugh Dubberly and Paul Pangaro, "On Modeling: What Is Conversation, and How Can We Design for It?," *Interactions* 16, no. 4 (2009): 22–28, https://doi.org/10.1145/1551986.1551991.

12. Mikhail Bakhtin, *The Dialogic Imagination: Four Essays*, University of Texas Press Slavic Series 1 (Austin: Univ. of Texas Press, 1981); L. S. Vygotskij, *Mind in Society: The Development of Higher Psychological Processes*, ed. Michael Cole et al. (Cambridge, MA: Harvard Univ. Press, 1978).

13. Jerome Bruner, "The Narrative Construction of Reality," *Critical Inquiry* 18, no. 1 (1991): 1–21, https://doi.org/10.1086/448619.

14. Louis Menand, *The Metaphysical Club: A Story of Ideas in America* (New York: Farrar, Straus & Giroux, 2001); Scott L. Pratt, *Native Pragmatism: Rethinking the Roots of American Philosophy* (Bloomington: Indiana Univ. Press, 2002).

15. Bohm, Factor, and Garrett, "Dialogue: A Proposal"

16. Bohm, Factor, and Garrett.

17. Dubberly and Pangaro, "On Modeling," 23.

18. Bohm, Factor, and Garrett, "Dialogue: A Proposal."

19. Jeffrey D. Ford, "Organizational Change as Shifting Conversations," *Journal of Organizational Change Management* 12, no. 6 (1999): 480, https://doi.org/10.1108/09534819910300855.

20. Barbara Czarniawska-Joerges, *Narrating the Organization: Dramas of Institutional Identity* (Chicago: Univ. of Chicago Press, 1997); Ramkrishnan V. Tenkasi, and Richard J. Boland Jr, "Locating Meaning Making in Organizational Learning: The Narrative Basis of Cognition," in *Research in Organizational Change and Development* 7 (1993): 77–103.

21. Gibson Burrell and Gareth Morgan, *Sociological Paradigms and Organisational Analysis: Elements of the Sociology of Corporate Life* (London: Routledge, 2016).

22. Peter L. Berger and Thomas Luckmann, *The Social Construction of Reality: A Treatise in the Sociology of Knowledge* (New York: Anchor Books, 1990); B. Holzner, *Reality Construction in Society* (Cambridge, MA: Schenkman, 1972); John R. Searle, *The Construction of Social Reality* (New York: Free Press, 1995); Paul Watzlawick,

The Invented Reality (W. W. Norton, 2011); W. Graham Astley, "Administrative Science as Socially Constructed Truth," *Administrative Science Quarterly* 30, no. 4 (1985): 497, https://doi.org/10.2307/2392694; Karl E. Weick, *Sensemaking in Organizations*, Foundations for Organizational Science (Thousand Oaks, CA: Sage, 1995).

23. Ford, "Organizational Change as Shifting Conversations," 480; See also Peter M. Senge, *The Fifth Discipline: The Art and Practice of the Learning Organization*, rev. ed. (New York: Doubleday/Currency, 2006); D. M. Boje, "Stories of the Storytelling Organization: A Postmodern Analysis of Disney as 'Tamara-Land,'" *Academy of Management Journal* 38, no. 4 (1995): 997-1035, https://doi.org/10.2307/256618; Tojo Thachankary, "Organizations as 'texts': Hermeneutics as a Model for Understanding Organizational Change," in *Research in Organizational Change and Development* 6, no. 2 (1992): 1997-233.

24. William G. Tierney and Michael Lanford, "Conceptualizing Innovation in Higher Education," in *Higher Education: Handbook of Theory and Research*, ed. Michael B. Paulsen, vol. 31, Higher Education: Handbook of Theory and Research (Cham: Springer International, 2016), 1-40, https://doi.org/10.1007/978-3-319-26829-3_1; David F. Labaree, *A Perfect Mess: The Unlikely Ascendancy of American Higher Education* (Chicago: Univ. of Chicago Press, 2017), https://doi.org/10.7208/chicago/9780226250588.001.0001; Rukhsar Sharif, "The Relations between Acculturation and Creativity and Innovation in Higher Education: A Systematic Literature Review," *Educational Research Review* 28 (Nov. 2019): 100287, https://doi.org/10.1016/j.edurev.2019.100287.

25. Maggie Berg and Barbara Karolina Seeber, *The Slow Professor: Challenging the Culture of Speed in the Academy* (Toronto: Univ. of Toronto Press, 2016).

26. Jake Knapp, John Zeratsky, and Braden Kowitz, *Sprint: How to Solve Big Problems and Test New Ideas in Just Five Days* (New York: Simon & Schuster, 2016).

27. Horst W. J. Rittel and Melvin M. Webber, "Dilemmas in a General Theory of Planning," *Policy Sciences* 4, no. 2 (1973): 155-69, https://doi.org/10.1007/BF01405730; Herbert A. Simon, "Applying Information Technology to Organization Design," *Public Administration Review* 33, no. 3 (1973): 268, https://doi.org/10.2307/974804.

28. C. West Churchman, "Free for All," *Management Science* 14, no. 4 (1967): B-141-B-146, https://doi.org/10.1287/mnsc.14.4.B141.

29. Knapp, Zeratsky, and Kowitz, *Sprint*, 15.

30. Jeffrey D. Ford and Laurie W. Ford, "The Role of Conversations in Producing Intentional Change in Organizations," *Academy of Management Review* 20, no. 3 (1995): 541-70, https://doi.org/10.5465/amr.1995.9508080330.

31. Allan L. Scherr, "Managing for Breakthroughs in Productivity," *Human Resource Management* 28, no. 3 (1989): 403-24, https://doi.org/10.1002/hrm.3930280308.

32. Terry Winograd and Fernando Flores, *Understanding Computers and Cognition: A New Foundation for Design* (Boston: Addison-Wesley, 2008).

33. Vijay Kumar, *101 Design Methods: A Structured Approach for Driving Innovation in Your Organization* (Hoboken, NJ: Wiley, 2013).

34. Kumar.

35. Grant P. Wiggins and Jay McTighe, *Understanding by Design*, 2nd ed., rev. (Alexandria, VA: Association for Supervision and Curriculum Development, 2005).

36. Knapp, Zeratsky, and Kowitz, *Sprint*.

37. Kevin Smith, "The Illusion of Design Sprints during a Global Pandemic" (Facebook Design, Aug. 12, 2020), https://medium.com/facebook-design/design -sprint-116634e83ff1.

38. Three types of conflict in particular occur in group conversations: relationship conflict (incompatibilities create friction), task conflict (groups members disagree about the task at hand), and process conflict (groups members disagree about how to and who should accomplish the task.) K. A. Jehn and E. A. Mannix, "The Dynamic Nature of Conflict: A Longitudinal Study of Intragroup Conflict and Group Performance," *Academy of Management Journal* 44, no. 2 (2001): 238–51, https://doi.org/10.2307/3069453.

39. Nigel Cross, *Design Thinking: Understanding How Designers Think and Work* (Oxford: Berg, 2011), 12, https://doi.org/10.5040/9781474293884.

40. Adam Connor and Aaron Irizarry, *Discussing Design: Improving Communication and Collaboration through Critique* (Sebastopol, CA: O'Reilly Media, 2015).

41. Thomas Wendt, *Design for Dasein: Understanding the Design of Experiences* (Charleston, SC: Createspace, 2015), 16.

42. James Kalbach, *Mapping Experiences: A Guide to Creating Value through Journeys, Blueprints, and Diagrams* (Sebastopol, CA: O'Reilly Media, 2016).

43. Wendt, *Design for Dasein*, 25.

44. David Factor, "On Facilitation and Purpose: An Open Letter," 1994, http:// www.david-bohm.net/dialogue/facilitation_purpose.html.

45. Nicholas C. Burbules, *Dialogue in Teaching: Theory and Practice* (New York: Teachers College Press, 1993).

46. Connor and Irizarry, *Discussing Design*.

47. Lorenzo Rocío et al., "The Mix that Matters: Innovation through Diversity" (Boston: Boston Consulting Group, 2017), https://www.bcg.com/en-us/publications /2017/people-organization-leadership-talent-innovation-through-diversity-mix -that-matters.

48. David G. Jansson and Steven M. Smith, "Design Fixation," *Design Studies* 12, no. 1 (1991): 3–11, https://doi.org/10.1016/0142-694X(91)90003-F; Evgeny Morozov, *To Save Everything, Click Here: The Folly of Technological Solutionism* (New York: PublicAffairs, 2013); and Sridhar Condoor and Donna LaVoie, "Design Fixation: A Cognitive Model" (Proceedings of the ICED, 16th International Conference on Engineering Design, Paris, France, July 28–31, 2007), https://www.designsociety .org/publication/25504/Design+Fixation%3A+a+Cognitive+Model.

49. Connor and Irizarry, *Discussing Design*.

50. Nathan Crilly, "Fixation and Creativity in Concept Development: The Attitudes and Practices of Expert Designers," *Design Studies* 38 (May 2015): 54–91, https://doi.org/10.1016/j.destud.2015.01.002.

51. David Bohm and F. David Peat, *Science, Order, and Creativity* (London: Routledge, 1989), 241.

52. Wendt, *Design for Dasein*.

53. J. S. Linsey et al., "A Study of Design Fixation, Its Mitigation and Perception in Engineering Design Faculty," *Journal of Mechanical Design* 132, no. 4 (2010): 041003, https://doi.org/10.1115/1.4001110; Diana P. Moreno et al., "A Step Beyond to Overcome Design Fixation: A Design-by-Analogy Approach," in *Design Computing and Cognition '14*, ed. John S. Gero and Sean Hanna (Cham: Springer International, 2015), 607–24, https://doi.org/10.1007/978-3-319-14956-1_34.

54. Factor, "On Facilitation and Purpose." Interestingly, Jeffrey D. Ford, Laurie W. Ford, and Angelo D'Amelio ("Resistance to Change: The Rest of the Story," *Academy of Management Review* 33, no. 2 [2008]: 362077) remind us that resistance views are typically "change-agent centric," that is, they take the side of those seeking to bring change—without recognizing that change agents contribute to resistance through their own actions. Instead, they argued three ways that change agents contribute to resistance to change: (1) by considering resistance as a self-fulfilling label given by change agents to make sense of others' reactions to change initiatives, (2) by their own actions or inactions that contribute to resistance, such as breach of agreement or lack of trust in relationship building, and (3) by failing to see resistance as both positive contribution to and momentum for change. Instead, they proposed to reconstruct resistance as the interaction between change recipients' behavior and response to change, the change agent's sense-making or interpretation of change recipients' actions, and the change agent-recipient relationship within which the first two elements occur to shape the interaction. "The change agent's job, therefore, must surely include responsibility for the relationship with recipients, as well as the tactics for change implementation. This includes taking charge of the change dialogues to include inquiry that gets to the root of apparently resistive behaviors by bringing both agent and recipient background conversations to the fore and engaging in those actions needed to maintain and improve the agent-client relationship" (373).

55. Michael Beer, *Organization Change and Development: A Systems View* (Santa Monica, CA: Goodyear, 1980); K. Morris and C. Raben, "The Fundamentals of Change Management," in *Discontinuous Change: Leading Organizational Transformation*, ed. David Nadler, Robert B. Shaw, and A. Elise Walton, Jossey-Bass Management Series (San Francisco: Jossey-Bass, 1995), 47–65; James O'Toole, *Leading Change: Overcoming the Ideology of Comfort and the Tyranny of Custom*, Jossey-Bass Management Series (San Francisco: Jossey-Bass, 1995); Allan M. Mohrman et al., "The Phenomenon of Large-Scale Organizational Change," in *Large-Scale Organizational Change*, Jossey-Bass Management Series (San Francisco: Jossey-Bass, 1989), 1–31; Chris Argyris, *Overcoming Organizational Defenses: Facilitating Organizational Learning* (Boston: Allyn & Bacon, 1990); Barry M. Staw, "The Escalation of Commitment to a Course of Action," *Academy of Management Review* 6, no. 4 (1981): 577–87, https://doi.org/10.5465/amr.1981.4285694.

56. Peter Block, *Stewardship: Choosing Service over Self-Interest*, 2nd ed., rev. (San Francisco: Berrett-Koehler, 2013); Senge, *The Fifth Discipline*; Morris and Raben, "The Fundamentals of Change Management"; O'Toole, *Leading Change*.

57. Carol O'Connor, "Managing Resistance to Change," *Management Development Review* 6, no. 4 (1993): 25.

58. Bohm, Factor, and Garrett, "Dialogue—A Proposal."

59. Connor and Irizarry, *Discussing Design*.

60. Jeffrey D. Ford, Laurie W. Ford, and Randall T. McNamara, "Resistance and the Background Conversations of Change," *Journal of Organizational Change Management* 15, no. 2 (2002): 105–21, https://doi.org/10.1108/09534810210422991.

61. Ford, Ford, and McNamara, 108. In that scenario, three types of conversational pattern impact resistance to change: complacency, resignation, and cynicism. Complacent background conversations refer to an organization's historical success, and people use these successes to justify leaving things as they are. Complacent resistance conversations, therefore, reflect a theme of "nothing new or different is needed." There is talk about relative comfort and satisfaction with the way things are, the way things are done, and their preferred continuation to ensure success in the future. Resigned background conversations are, on the opposite, built on historical failures and have resigned people to having no hope for change. Resigned resistance conversations, in addition to expressing discouragement or even hopelessness, contain the suggestion that another individual or organization would likely succeed, even in these very same circumstances. Finally, cynical background conversations also emerge from historical failures, but as understood through other narratives, not through direct experience. Cynical resistance conversations reflect a distrust and disbelief in others.

62. Ford, Ford, and McNamara, 114.

Chapter 4. Change Management as Design

1. Tim Brown and Barry Katz, "Change by Design," *Journal of Product Innovation Management* 28, no. 3 (2011): 328, https://doi.org/10.1111/j.1540-5885.2011.00806.x

2. Deborah Rowland, *Still Moving: How to Lead Mindful Change* (Chichester, UK: Wiley Blackwell, 2017).

3. Rowland, 12.

4. Kurt Lewin, *Field Theory in Social Science: Selected Theoretical Papers* (New Delhi: Isha Books, 2013).

5. Mark Michaels, *The Quest for Fitness: A Rational Exploration into the New Science of Organization* (San Jose, CA: Writers Club Press, 2000); Ronald Lippitt, Jeanne Watson, and Bruce Westley, *The Dynamics of Planned Change: A Comparative Study of Principles and Techniques* (New York: Harcourt Brace, 1958); Edgar H. Schein and Warren G. Bennis, *Personal and Organizational Change through Group Methods: The Laboratory Approach* (New York: Wiley, 1965); David A. Kolb and Alan L. Frohman, *Organizational Development through Planned Change: A Development Model* (London: Franklin Classics, 2018); Noel M. Tichy and Mary Anne

Devanna, *The Transformational Leader: The Key to Global Competitiveness*, A Wiley Management Classic (New York: Wiley, 1990); John Kotter, "Leading Change: Why Transformation Efforts Fail," *Harvard Business Review* 73, no. 2 (1995): 59–67; Edgar H. Schein, *Organizational Culture and Leadership*, 5th ed. (Hoboken, NJ: Wiley, 2017).

6. Bernard Burnes, "Kurt Lewin and the Planned Approach to Change: A Re-Appraisal," *Journal of Management Studies* 41, no. 6 (2004): 977–1002, https://doi.org/10.1111/j.1467-6486.2004.00463.x.

7. Paul S. Goodman and Lance Kurke, "Studies of Change in Organizations: A Status Report," in *Change in Organizations: New Perspectives on Theory, Research, and Practice*, ed. Paul S. Goodman, Jossey-Bass Social and Behavioral Science Series (San Francisco: Jossey-Bass, 1982).

8. James Paul Gee, *The Anti-Education Era: Creating Smarter Students through Digital Learning* (New York: Palgrave Macmillan, 2013), 88.

9. Rune Todnem, "Organisational Change Management: A Critical Review," *Journal of Change Management* 5, no. 4 (2005): 550, https://doi.org/10.1080/14697010500359250.

10. Mark Hughes, "Do 70 Per Cent of All Organizational Change Initiatives Really Fail?," *Journal of Change Management* 11, no. 4 (2011): 451–64, https://doi.org/10.1080/14697017.2011.630506. Hughes challenges this figure.

11. Kotter, "Leading Change"; John P. Kotter, *Leading Change* (Boston: Harvard Business Review Press, 2012).

12. Dean Anderson and Linda S. Ackerman-Anderson, *Beyond Change Management: How to Achieve Breakthrough Results through Conscious Change Leadership*, Pfeiffer Essential Resources for Training and HR Professionals, 2nd ed. (San Francisco: Pfeiffer, 2010).

13. Factor, Donald, "On Facilitation and Purpose: An Open Letter," 1994, http://www.david-bohm.net/dialogue/facilitation_purpose.html.

14. Kotter, *Leading Change*.

15. Wanda J. Orlikowski and J. Debra Hofman, "An Improvisational Model for Change Management: The Case of Groupware Technologies," *Sloan Management Review*, 38, no. 2 (1997): 12.

16. Fiona Graetz and Aaron C. T. Smith, "Managing Organizational Change: A Philosophies of Change Approach," *Journal of Change Management* 10, no. 2 (2010): 136, https://doi.org/10.1080/14697011003795602. We said Lewin was important. The freezing-unfreezing pattern is persistent.

17. Todnem, "Organisational Change Management," 375.

18. Bryan J. Weiner, "A Theory of Organizational Readiness for Change," in *Handbook on Implementation Science*, ed. Per Nilsen and Sarah Birken (Cheltenham, UK: Edward Elgar, 2020), 215–32, https://doi.org/10.4337/9781788975995.00015.

19. Weiner, 227.

20. Weiner, 219.

21. Icek Ajzen, "The Theory of Planned Behavior," *Organizational Behavior and Human Decision Processes* 50, no. 2 (1992): 179–211.

22. Graetz and Smith, "Managing Organizational Change," 135–54, https://doi.org/10.1080/14697011003795602.

23. Graetz and Smith, 137.

24. Anderson and Ackerman-Anderson, *Beyond Change Management*, 116.

25. Graetz and Smith, "Managing Organizational Change," 136.

26. Graetz and Smith, 148.

27. Rachel Cooper, Sabine Junginger, and Thomas Lockwood, eds., *The Handbook of Design Management* (London: Bloomsbury Academic, 2011), 188.

28. Alessandro Deserti and Francesca Rizzo, "Design and the Cultures of Enterprises," *Design Issues* 30, no. 1 (2014): 36, https://doi.org/10.1162/DESI_a_00247.

29. Denish Shah et al., "The Path to Customer Centricity," *Journal of Service Research* 9, no. 2 (2006): 113–24, https://doi.org/10.1177/1094670506294666.

30. Deserti and Rizzo, "Design and the Cultures of Enterprises," 36.

31. Deserti and Rizzo, 36–37.

32. Deserti and Rizzo, 54.

33. Deserti and Rizzo, 55.

34. Adrienne M. Brown, *Emergent Strategy* (Chico, CA: AK Press, 2017).

35. For more, see Jon Kolko, "Design Thinking Comes of Age" (Harvard Business Publishing, 2015).

36. Rowland, *Still Moving*.

37. Rowland.

38. Building trust as part of design processes is such an important issue, and of course, it is integral to effective leadership. Trust is both a precondition and an outcome of codesign (Marika Lüders et al., eds., *Innovating for Trust* [Cheltenham, UK: Edward Elgar, 2017]). More generally, organizational scientists argue that inter- and intraorganizational trust is the key component to stimulate collaboration and creativity and to foster innovation (Anna Brattström, Hans Löfsten, and Anders Richtnér, "Creativity, Trust and Systematic Processes in Product Development," *Research Policy* 41, no. 4 (2012): 743–55, https://doi.org/10.1016/j.respol.2011.12.003.

Chapter 5. Assessment and Research in a Higher Education Design Organization

1. Donna M. Mertens, "Transformative Paradigm: Mixed Methods and Social Justice," *Journal of Mixed Methods Research* 1, no. 3 (2007): 212–25, https://doi.org/10.1177/1558689807302811.

2. Peter T. Ewell, "An Emerging Scholarship: A Brief History of Assessment," in *Building a Scholarship of Assessment*, ed. Trudy W. Banta (San Francisco: Jossey-Bass, 2010), 3–25.

3. Linda A. Suskie, *Assessing Student Learning: A Common Sense Guide*, Jossey-Bass Higher and Adult Education Series, 2nd ed. (San Francisco: Jossey-Bass, 2009).

4. Ernest L. Boyer, *Scholarship Reconsidered: Priorities of the Professoriate* (Law-

renceville, NJ: Princeton Univ. Press, 1990), https://eric.ed.gov/?id=ED326149; National Research Council, *Discipline-Based Education Research: Understanding and Improving Learning in Undergraduate Science and Engineering* (Washington, DC: National Academies Press, 2012), https://doi.org/10.17226/13362.

5. Karl E. Weick, "Educational Organizations as Loosely Coupled Systems," *Administrative Science Quarterly* 21, no. 1 (1976): 1, https://doi.org/10.2307/2391875.

6. Weick, 6–9.

7. Lee G. Bolman and Terrence E. Deal, *Reframing Organizations: Artistry, Choice, and Leadership*, 6th ed. (Hoboken, NJ: Jossey-Bass, 2017).

8. Libby Hoffman, "45 Design Thinking Exercises You Can Use Today," 2019, https://blog.prototypr.io/45-design-thinking-exercises-91bf63d2ef15. Graphic used with permission. Libby is a recent graduate of MSU and was a student employee in the Hub from 2016 to 2017. At the same time, Libby worked with Design for America, a registered student organization at MSU, and brought her design experience to the Hub, where she supported several projects with systems thinking graphics and data analysis. Libby co-led the Hub's inaugural Student Design Team in the academic year 2016/17.

9. Donald L. Kirkpatrick and James D. Kirkpatrick, *Evaluating Training Programs: The Four Levels*, 3rd ed. (San Francisco: Berrett-Koehler, 2006); Ashley Finley, "A Comprehensive Approach to Assessment of High-Impact Practices." Occasional Paper no. 41 (Washington, DC: National Institute for Learning Outcomes Assessment, 2019), https://eric.ed.gov/?id=ED604467.

10. Daniel L. Reinholz and Tessa C. Andrews, "Change Theory and Theory of Change: What's the Difference Anyway?," *International Journal of STEM Education* 7, no. 1 (2020): 2, https://doi.org/10.1186/s40594-020-0202-3.

11. Jaime Lester, *Learning Analytics in Higher Education: Current Innovations, Future Potential, and Practical Applications* (New York: Routledge, 2018), https://doi.org/10.4324/9780203731864.

12. Barbara S. Bonham and Hunter R. Boylan, "Developmental Mathematics: Challenges, Promising Practices, and Recent Initiatives," *Journal of Developmental Education* 34, no. 3 (2011): 2.

13. Samuel L. Tunstall et al., "Quantitative Literacy at Michigan State University, 3: Designing General Education Mathematics Courses," *Numeracy* 9, no. 2 (2016): 6, https://doi.org/10.5038/1936-4660.9.2.6.

14. National Academies of Sciences, Engineering, and Medicine, *Barriers and Opportunities for 2-Year and 4-Year STEM Degrees: Systemic Change to Support Students' Diverse Pathways*, ed. Shirley Malcom and Michael Feder (Washington, DC: National Academies Press, 2016), https://doi.org/10.17226/21739.

15. Samuel L. Tunstall, Rebecca L. Matz, and Jeffrey C. Craig, "Quantitative Literacy Courses as a Space for Fusing Literacies," *Journal of General Education* 65, no. 3 (2016): 178–94, https://muse.jhu.edu/article/687339; Younggon Bae et al., "Alignment Between Learning Objectives and Assessments in a Quantitative Literacy Course," *Numeracy* 12, no. 2 (2019): 10, https://doi.org/10.5038/1936-4660

.12.2.10; Rebecca L. Matz and Samuel L. Tunstall, "Embedded Remediation Is Not Necessarily a Pathway for Equitable Access to Quantitative Literacy and College Algebra: Results from a Pilot Study," *Numeracy* 12, no. 2 (2019): 3, https://doi.org /10.5038/1936-4660.12.2.3.

16. Hannah Farrimond, *Doing Ethical Research* (London: Macmillan Education UK, 2013); Rachel Brooks, Kitty te Riele, and Meg Maguire, *Ethics and Education Research* (London: SAGE Publications, 2014), https://doi.org/10.4135 /9781473909762.

17. Warren I. Susman, *Culture as History: The Transformation of American Society in the Twentieth Century* (Washington, DC: Smithsonian Institution Press, 2003).

18. Ellen Sue Stern, *I Do: Meditations for Brides* (New York: Dell, 1993).

19. Jason A. Springs, *Toward a Generous Orthodoxy* (Oxford: Oxford Univ. Press, 2010), https://doi.org/10.1093/acprof:oso/9780195395044.001.0001.

20. Kate Bridges and Michael Woolcock, *How (Not) to Fix Problems That Matter: Assessing and Responding to Malawi's History of Institutional Reform*, Policy Research Working Papers (Washington, DC: World Bank, 2017), https://doi.org/10.1596/1813 -9450-8289.

Chapter 6. Designing Requires a Design Organization

1. Donna M. Mertens, "Transformative Paradigm: Mixed Methods and Social Justice," *Journal of Mixed Methods Research* 1, no. 3 (2007): 212–25, https://doi.org /10.1177/1558689807302811.

2. Clay Spinuzzi, *All Edge: Inside the New Workplace Networks* (Chicago: Univ. of Chicago Press, 2015), 23

3. Spinuzzi, 27.

4. Dave Malouf, "Introducing DesignOps," in *DesignOps Handbook*, ed. Gregg Bernstein (InVision, 2019), 19, https://www.designbetter.co/designops-handbook.

5. Malouf, 18.

6. Malouf, 19–22.

7. Fabricio Teixeira, "DesignOps: The Questions You're Probably Asking Yourself Now," *Medium* (blog), June 24, 2018, https://uxdesign.cc/designops-the -questions-youre-probably-asking-yourself-now-fdac491bfe4f.

8. Colin Whitehead, "DesignOps Scenarios and Models," in Bernstein, *DesignOps Handbook*, 37, https://www.designbetter.co/designops-handbook.

9. Peter Merholz and Kristin Skinner, *Org Design for Design Orgs: Building and Managing In-House Design Teams* (Sebastopol, CA: O'Reilly Media, 2016), vii.

10. Dave Malouf et al., "DesignOps Canvas," *Gamestorming* (blog), Dec. 13, 2017, https://gamestorming.com/mapping-design-operations/.

11. Merholz and Skinner, *Org Design for Design Orgs*.

12. Malouf et al., "DesignOps Canvas," 4.

13. Merholz and Skinner, *Org Design for Design Orgs*, 9–20.

14. Steven A. Stolz, "Embodied Learning," *Educational Philosophy and Theory* 47, no. 5 (2015): 474–87.

15. In Seth Chaiklin's "The Zone of Proximal Development in Vygotsky's Analysis of Learning and Instruction," in *Vygotsky's Educational Theory in Cultural Context*, ed. Alex Kozulin et al. (Cambridge: Cambridge Univ. Press, 2003), 39–64, https://doi.org/10.1017/CBO9780511840975.004.

16. Jerome S. Bruner, *The Process of Education* (Cambridge, MA: Harvard Univ. Press, 1977).

17. Merholz and Skinner, *Org Design for Design Orgs*, 8.

18. Malouf, "Introducing DesignOps," 7.

19. Malouf, 7.

INDEX

academic achievement, 3; during COVID-19 pandemic, 140–41; and credit completion level, 116–17; learning analytics analysis project, 115–17; as project goal, 114–15. *See also* graduation rate

academic disciplines: discipline-based educational research (DBER), 24; ranked faculty, 146n29; siloed structure, 30, 44, 65, 125, 126–27, 128

academic freedom, 37

accountability, 21, 59, 88, 98–99, 105–6, 113

accountability model, of change management, 88–89

Ackerman-Anderson, Linda S., 88, 93

action research, 86

active learning, 70, 98

adaptive learning, 19

adhocracy, 115; all-edge, 126–32

ADKAR model, of change management, 86–87, 88

alignment diagrams, 76–77

American Council on Education, 1–2

analogical observation, 81

Anderson, Dean, 88–89, 93

app development project, 53–59

app economy, 55

Apple, 70, 95; *Everyone Can Code* curriculum, 54, 57; iOS Design Lab project and, 53–59; Swift programming language, 54–59

argumentation, 64, 68, 80

Arizona State University, 19

Asana software, 113, 125

assessment, in design organizations, 21–22, 105–23; definition, 106–7; ethical considerations, 119–23; in loosely cou-

pled systems, 107–10; organizational uses, 115–19; tactical uses, 110–15

Association of Veterinary Medical Colleges (AAVMC), 96

autonomy, 4–5, 26, 35, 39, 107–8

backward design planning, 72–73

Bass, Randy, 6

Bohm, David, 65–66, 68

"boot camps," 103–4

bottom-up approach, 94

Bowen, William, 3

brain storming, 50, 70

British Design Council, Double Diamond design process, 48–49. *See also* double-diamond design process

Brody, David Eric, 44

Brown, Brené, 53

Brown, Tim, 53

Buchanan, Richard, 9, 70–71

bureaucracies, 126–27

Campbell, Chris, 27

case studies, 114

challenge-based learning (CBL), 54, 55, 67, 69–70

challenges, to higher education, 1–2

change: theory of, 110–11, 113. *See also* institutional/organizational change

change agents, 69, 81–82, 139–40, 141, 152n54

change management, 2, 16, 84–104, 141; action research, 86; components, 85–92; as conversation design framework, 66, 67, 69; as core competency, 87–88; as design, 21, 92–96; field theory, 86; group dynamics, 86; models and theories, 87–89; organizational psychology

change management (*cont.*)
component, 85, 87, 89; planned or emergent approach, 90, 93, 103; processes, 89; as project management, 91–92; rational change model, 91–93; readiness for change, 86–87, 90–91; research fundamentals, 85–92; at scale, 18; in student experience design project, 102–3; top-down approach, 94–95

change management outcomes measurement. *See* assessment, in design organizations

change resistance, 46, 94, 152n54; conversation design and, 78, 81–83, 153n61

Clark, Hazel, 44

cocurricular projects, 34, 36, 110, 112, 121

coding, in iOS Design Lab project, 53–59

collaboration, 14, 115, 138, 155n38; in conversation design, 10–11, 68–69; in design operationalization, 51–52, 58–59; digital, 125, 131, 137, 138; goals, 18; interdisciplinary, 23–24, 58–59, 65, 123; in iOS Design Lab project, 54, 55, 58–59; in learning experience design, 26, 51, 52

community colleges, 5

competency-based education (CBE), 96–97, 98, 99

Conference on Systematic and Intuitive Methods in Engineering, Industrial Design, Architecture and Communication, 45

conversation analyses, 66–67

conversation design, 10–12, 20–21, 42, 47, 62–63, 64–83; activities, 73, 74, 75–77, 78; background conversations, 82–83; change management framework, 66, 67, 69; change resistance and, 78, 81–83, 153n61; for closure, 71; constructivist approach, 66, 67–69, 82–83, 141; cultural normativity, 65–66, 67, 68; definition, 64; design sprint methodology, 66, 67, 69–71; equity, diversity, and inclusion in, 78–79; ethical, collaborative, innovative, and responsible aspects, 66; facilitation in, 73–74, 77–78; fixed design solutions, 79–81; French program redesign, 71–78; for initiative, 71; intent statements, 76; interdisciplinary approach, 66–67; learning experience

basis, 67; mini design brief, 76; for performance, 71; power and organizational theory, 64–65; problem-solving component, 67, 69–70; resistance to change and, 78, 81–83; situating, 66–71; space for, 73, 74–76, 78; threats to, 78–83; for understanding, 71, 72–73

Conway, J., 46

Cooper, Rachel, 16

core competency, design as, 3, 6–7, 141

cost pressures, in higher education, 1–2

COVID-19 pandemic, 2, 11, 57, 65, 75, 140–41, 230; remote learning and teaching during, 60–61, 124–26

creativity, 2, 13, 30, 31, 45, 50, 103, 136–37, 155n38; in app design, 56–57; conversation design and, 66, 68, 80–81, 83; deconstructive, 139; double-diamond design process and, 50, 62; infrastructures for, 103; vulnerability and, 52

credit momentum campaign, 116–17

Crilly, Nathan, 80

Cross, Nigel, 76

curriculum: mathematics, 117–19; "spiral," 133; veterinary medicine, 21, 96–102

cybernetics, 10, 66–67

Dalziel, James, 27

data-driven interactive research, 86

Davidson, Cathy, 3–4, 6

decentralization, 4–5, 33, 107–8, 115

decision-making, 7–8, 21, 32, 105, 115–16, 123, 131, 141–42

demographic trends, 1–2, 87

Deserti, Alessandro, 94–95, 101

design: as core competency, 3, 6–7, 141; goals, 67, 93; historical need for, 3–4; language and terminology of, 9–12; potential for, 5

design culture, 94–96, 101–2, 139–40

design mindset, 94

DesignOps, 22, 128–32; collaborative approach, 132; goal, mission, and purpose, 128–29, 131; Hub for Innovation in Learning and Technology, 22, 128–32; professional development process, 132–39

design organizations, 15–17, 124–42; as all-edge adhocracies, 126–32; as change agents, 139–40; learning component, 132–39. *See also* Hub for Innovation in Learning and Technology

design sprints, 125; in assessment and research, 120; in conversation design, 66, 67, 69–71, 75; in COVID-19 pandemic response, 140–41; equity and, 79

design thinking, 43, 44–46, 52, 63, 70, 84, 95

Design Thinking (Rowe), 45

Development Operations (DevOps), 128

digital collaboration, 125, 131, 137, 138

digital economy, iOS Design Lab project, 53–59

digital photography, 29–30

digital student experience, 102

digital tools, 131

discipline-based educational research (DBER), 24

Disney, 15

dissension and conflict, 75, 121

diversity, 18, 34, 58, 70, 115–16, 208; in conversation design, 78–80; in student orientation programs, 35–36

Dobozy, Eva, 27

double-diamond design process, 48–52, 129–30, 131, 132; close phase, 49, 51, 57–58, 61; define phase, 49, 50, 55, 58, 60, 61, 70; deliver phase, 49, 50–51, 56–57, 58, 61, 70; development phase, 49, 50, 55–56, 58, 59, 61, 70; discover phase, 49, 54–55, 58, 59, 60, 61; funnel phase, 49, 58, 59, 61; impact, 49, 50, 58, 59, 61; input and output, 58, 59, 61; iterative implementation of solutions, 56–57, 63

educational attainment rates. *See* academic achievement

educational technologies, 1–2

Ellis, Manuel, 11

entrepreneurship, iOS Design Lab project, 53–59

equity, 12; as conversation design component, 78–80; as innovation, 17–19; as transition-to-college program component, 33, 35–36

Equity Design Collaborative, 79

ethics, in assessment and research activities, 119–23

evaluations, 13, 72, 99, 106, 113, 114, 206

experiential learning, 20, 28, 36, 58

extracurricular activities, 31, 120

Factor, Donald, 89, 152n54

faculty: Online Professional Development Design Project, 60–62; role in higher education change, 2; tenured/tenure-track, 38

field theory, 86

first-generation students, 17–18, 116; transition-to-college program, 35–36

Floor, Niels, 27–28

Floyd, George, 11

focus groups, 110, 114

Ford, Jeffrey D., 69, 71, 82

Ford, Laurie W., 71, 82

foundational change theory, 86–88

Frei, Hans, 121

"functional silo syndrome," 65

futures thinking, 43, 44, 47

Garrett, Peter, 65–66, 68

Gee, James Paul, 86

Georgia Institute of Technology, 1–2

Georgia State University, 19

GI Bill, 5

goals, measured against outcomes, 113

Google Docs, 131

Google Ventures Sprint method, 70–71

graduation rate, 13, 144n33; and credit completion level, 116–17; student success initiatives for, 18–19

Graetz, Fiona, 87, 90, 91–93

group conversations, conflict in, 75, 151n38

group dynamics, in change management, 86

higher education: exclusivity, 1; hierarchical nature, 1, 5, 130–31; historical development, 3–5

Hoffman, Libby, 110, 111, 156n8

Hofman, J. Debra, 90

Horizon Report, 26, 36

Hub for Innovation in Learning and Technology, 2–3, 8, 10, 13–17, 39; agile work approaches, 131; as all-edge adhocracy, 126–32; assessment and

Hub for Innovation in Learning and Technology (*cont.*)
research activities, 105–6, 107–10; as boundary-spanning unit, 108–9; collaborative nature, 18, 125; College of Veterinary Medicine Curriculum Redesign Project, 96–102; contextual commitments, 28–29; core management team, 131; design teams, 130–31, 138–39; equity imperative, 17–18; expertise, 130; framework, 129; French program redesign, 71–78; human-centered design approach, 79; institutional critique framework, 8–9; iOS Design Lab, 53–59; Learning Analytics Group (LAG), 115–17; learning experience design foundation, 28–29; logic models, 113; loosely coupled organizations and, 108–9; main street experience redesign, 133–39; mathematics department curricular partnership, 117–19; multidisciplinary approach, 132; Neighborhoods concept, 19; professional development projects, 60–61, 132–34; project outcome measurement, 113–15; as projects-based organization, 14–15; purpose, 139; relationship with partnering units, 122; remote learning and teaching activities, 60–62, 124–26; Student Design Team, 156n8; student experience design project, 102–4; student information system (SIS), 59–60; team culture, 125; as "third space," 13, 14, 73, 75, 105–6, 108–9, 122; University Innovation Alliance (UIA), 18–19. *See also* DesignOps; double-diamond design process
human-centered design process, 42–43, 48–49, 79, 114
human experience, as design process focus, 29, 31, 39, 51–52, 102
humanism, 135
Huron Consulting Group, 1–2

IBM, 95
ideation, 12, 45, 51, 77, 110, 111
IDEO, 45, 48–49, 53, 70
inclusion, 18, 35–36, 64–65, 78–80, 85, 119
innovation, 2, 6, 36–37, 45, 64, 141; design culture and, 94–96; equity as, 17–19;

faculty's lack of support for, 38; institutional change for, 39; resistance to, 94; service *vs.*, 14–15; threats to, 38
innovation hubs, 2. *See also* Hub for Innovation in Learning and Technology
"innovation theater," 45
Inside Higher Education (Mintz), 1–2, 13–14
institutional critique, 7–9
institutional/organizational change, 6–7, 16, 21, 69, 85, 114, 127; change management and, 85–86, 90, 91, 93–96; as continuum, 92, 93; design culture for, 94–96; disciplinarity as alternative to, 39; functions, 2; infrastructures, 93; leadership, 86, 87–88; outcomes, 93–94; short- and long-term goals, 121–22; stages, 88; unfreezing-change-refreezing process, 86–87, 90, 92. *See also* change management
instructional design, 25–26
intentional learning, 23
interdisciplinary approach: of all-edge adhocracies, 127, 128; collaborative, 23–24, 58–59, 65, 123; in conversation design, 66–67; in LXD, 36–39
interventionists, 77
interviews, 72, 110, 111, 114, 135, 137
iOS Design Lab, 53–59
iterative processes, 1, 9, 17, 103, 113, 114, 131, 133–34; in assessment and research activities, 114; in design operationalization, 48–49, 50–51, 56–59; double-diamond design process, 56–57, 63, 131; iOS Design Lab project, 56–59; as ongoing improvements, 122; physical space redesign, 133–34; as "spiral" curriculum, 133

Junginger, Sabine, 16

Kezar, Adrianna, 5
Kilgore, Whitney, 25–26
Kim, Joshua, *Learning Innovation and the Future of Education*, 5–6, 7, 8, 36, 37, 39
knowledge, communication of, 67
Kotter, John, 88, 89

Labaree, David, 4–5, 7
land-grant institutions, 5

landscape analyses, 110
Largent, Mark, 11
Laurilland, Diana, 27–28
leadership, 2; in change management, 84–85, 86, 103; change mindset of, 102–3; design leaders, 129; as design organization support, 131; of learning design, 36–37; in organizational change, 86, 87–88; in veterinary curriculum redesign project, 99, 100, 101
learning, as design component, 103
learning analytics, 27, 115–17
learning and teaching centers, 5, 13–14
learning designers, 36–37, 131–32, 141
learning engineers, 23–24
learning experience, 47
learning experience design (LXD), 18, 20–21, 23–41; discipline-based approach, 24, 36–39; instructional design relationship, 25–26; MSU College Transition Project, 32–36; patterns, 137; playbook, 137–38; in practice, 53–59; purpose-based, 26–27, 40–41; World of Experience Design (Floor), 27–28
Learning Innovation and the Future of Education (Kim and Maloney), 5–6, 7, 8, 36, 37, 39
learning organizations, 46–47
Lewin, Kurt, 85
Linsey, J. S., 81
logic models, 110–13
loosely coupled systems, 107–10, 122
Lorenzo, Rocío, 78
LXD. See learning experience design

Madsbjerg, Christian, 40; The Moment of Clarity, 29–30; Sensemaking, 30–31
Maloney, Edward, Learning Innovation and the Future of Education, 5–6, 7, 8, 36, 37, 39
Malouf, Dave, 128, 131, 139
management science, 29–30, 85
Manzini, Ezio, 9
Map of Design Methods (Hoffman), 110, 111
mapping activities, 50, 56, 70, 72, 73, 76, 81, 137
Massachusetts Institute of Technology (MIT): Online Education Policy Initiative report, 23–24; Systems Dynamic Group, 46
Masters, J., 46
mathematics department, revised curricular pathway, 117–19
Mau, Bruce, 84
McNamara, Randall T., 82
McPherson, Michael, 3
Meadows, Donella H., 46–47
mentoring and advising, 11–12; proactive, 19
Merholz, Peter, 129, 130, 135
Meyer, Angela, 16–17
Michigan State University (MSU): College Transition Project, 32–36; credit momentum campaign, 116–17; French program redesign, 71–78; graduation rate, 116–17, 144n33; iOS Design Lab, 20; Learning Analytics Group (LAG), 115–17; marginalizing policies, 11–12; remote learning and teaching, 124–26; student success initiative, 18–19. See also Hub for Innovation in Learning and Technology
Michigan State University, College of Veterinary Medicine curriculum reform, 21
Microsoft Teams, 131
Milev, Yana, 44
Mintz, Steven, 1–2, 13–14
Moment of Clarity, The (Madsbjerg and Rasmussen), 29–30
Moner, William, 3
Montgomery, Beronda, 11–12
Moreno, Diana P., 81
Morley, Louise, 65
morphological charts, 81
Morrill Act, 5
Motley, Phillip, 3
Mural (virtual whiteboard), 125, 131, 140

narratives, 65, 67, 153n61
National Research Council, 24
Nicolettou, Angela, 25–26

objectives, 80; in curriculum reform, 97–98; in loosely coupled systems, 110; process-based, 113; project-level, 114–15

observations, 57, 110, 111, 135, 137; analogical, 81
O'Connor, Carol, 82
Online Professional Development Design Project, 60–62
operationalization, of LXD, 42–63, 141; futures thinking component, 44, 47; Hub Design Process, 48–53; human-centered design component, 42–43; iOS Design Lab, 53–59; learning sciences component, 42; principles, 42–43; reflective moments in, 52–53; systems thinking component, 44, 46–47; transparency, 51–53
opportunity identification, 2
organizational change. *See* institutional/organizational change
organizational culture, 24, 88–89
organizational psychology, 85, 87, 89
orientation programs, MSU College Transition Project, 32–36
Orlikowski, Wanda J., 90
outcomes: assessment or research-based, 121–22; educational, 3; of organizational change, 93–94; of projects, 113–14; in student learning, 114–15

Pangero, Paul, 10
Papanek, Victor, 45
pedagogical metamodels, 27
phenomenology, 30, 32
playbooks, 137–38
Pope-Ruark, Rebecca, 3
precollege/bridge programs, 19, 32–36
problem-framing, 132, 135
problem solution paradox, 81
problem-solving: with action research, 86; in all-edge adhocracies, 128; with analogical observation, 81; for app economy, 55; challenge-based, 67, 69–70; with conversation design, 67, 69–70, 75; creative, 55, 58–59; with design thinking, 45; group-based, 75; humanizing of, 51–52; iterative, 2; as solutionism, 48, 79–81; "wicked" (complex) problems, 44, 70–71, 126–27
product development, 94–95
professional development projects, 140; define activities, 133; discovery activities, 133; learning approach, 133; main street experience redesign project, 133–39; for veterinary medicine faculty, 98
program evaluations, 114
project boards, 125, 136
project management practices, 131
Prosci, 87
prototyping, 52, 62, 70, 81, 103; in assessment and research activities, 110, 113, 120; in challenge-based learning, 54; in change management, 103, 110; in conversation design, 12, 70, 71, 77, 81; curricular, 56; in iOS Design Lab, 54, 58–59; LXD designers' role, 131–32; in physical space redesign, 136–37; in professional development project, 135, 136–37; rapid, 120, 131
provosts, 13, 14, 39, 101, 117, 131, 141
public education, defunding, 1–2

quantitative literacy, 118–19
question-driven approach, 110

Rangarajan, Nandhini, 48
Rasmussen, Mikkel B., *The Moment of Clarity*, 29–30
rational change model, 91–93
reality: constructed, 82, 83; conversation-based perception, 68, 69
regional state universities, 5
relationships, 30, 79, 82, 109, 120, 137, 139; change resistance and, 81–82; for conversation design, 81; for operationalization of design, 46, 51–52, 58; power-based, 122
remote learning and teaching, 60–62, 124–26
research, in design organizations, 21–22, 105–23; definition, 106, 107; discipline-based, 107; ethical considerations, 119–23; in loosely coupled systems, 107–10; organizational uses, 115–19; role in LXD, 27–28; tactical uses, 110–15
research universities: faculty attitudes toward LXD, 38; status, 5
resistant behaviors, 82
Rhetoric and Composition, 37–38

rhetoric/rhetorical action and practice, 7–9, 10, 67
Rittel, Horst, 45
Rizzo, Francesca, 94–95, 101
Rowland, Deborah, 84–85, 102–3

Sawyer, Diane, 120
scrums, 131
Seitzinger, Joyce, 25–26
Senge, Peter M., 46–47
Sensemaking (Madsbjerg), 30–31
serendipity, by design, 139
service design, 36
Shields, Patricia, 48
signage, 136–37
silos, 13–14, 20, 140; academic disciplines as, 30, 44, 65, 125, 126–27, 128
Simon, Herbert, 3, 24, 45
Skinner, Kristin, 129, 130, 135
Slack software, 131
Smith, Aaron C. T., 87, 90, 91–93
Smith, Kevin, 75
Smith, Martin, 23–24
social stratification, 64–65
Soulis, Spiros, 25–26
spatial thinking, 7
Spinuzzi, Clay, 126–27
Sprint (Knapp, Zeratsky, and Kowitz), 70, 74
staff, role in higher education change, 2
stakeholders, 2, 130, 140; in assessment and research activities, 110, 113; in change management, 85; conversation design with, 63, 80, 82; in loosely coupled systems, 106, 108; in LXD, 42–43; multiple, 103; needs assessment, 110; in operationalization of design, 48, 50, 52, 53, 55, 56, 62; in transition-to-college programs, 33, 34
standups, 131, 136
Stanford d.School, 45, 48–49, 78–79
STEM degree programs, 119
storytelling, 53, 59, 136
stratification, of higher education, 5
structural-functionalism, 69
student information system (SIS), 59–60
students: role in higher education change, 2; as stakeholders, 130; transition-to-college programs, 19, 32–36

student success. *See* academic achievement
surveys, 1, 61, 107, 114
Suskie, Linda, 107
Swift programming language, 54–59
systems design, 27
systems thinking, 43, 44, 46–47, 49, 85, 141, 156n8

Taylor, Breonna, 11
teaching outcomes, 3
Teal, Randall, 48
teamwork, 54, 55, 56, 58–59, 77–78, 132, 137
Theory of Planned Behavior (Ajzen), 91
"third space," innovation hubs as, 13, 14, 73, 75, 105–6, 108–9, 122
Thorold, J., 46
Todnem, Rune, 87–88, 90
top-down approach, 44, 85, 92, 94–95
transformative process, of higher education, 2
transparency, 34, 51, 59, 82, 102
trust, 105–6, 121, 152n54, 155n38; change management and, 101, 103; conversation design and, 75, 79; within loosely coupled systems, 108
"turn to learning" initiative, 5–6

unfreezing-change-refreezing process, of organizational change, 86–87, 90, 92
universities, as loosely coupled systems, 107–10
University of Florida, 19
user experience (UX) methods, 27

vendors, 115
veterinary medicine, curriculum redesign project, 96–102; change management aspect, 98, 100, 101–2; competency-based education basis, 96–97, 98, 99; faculty involvement, 98–100; implications, 98–102; leadership, 99, 100, 101; objectives, 97; outcomes, 98; professional development component, 97, 99; sustainability, 97, 98, 100–101
video conferencing, 75, 125, 131, 140
vulnerability, 52–53
Vygotsky, Lev, 133

Webber, Melvin, 45
Weick, Karl, 107–8
Weiner, Bryan J., 90–91
Wendt, Thomas, 28, 52, 77, 81
whiteboards, 45, 74, 76, 124, 125, 131, 140

Yale Report of 1928, 5

zone of proximal development, 133
zones of ambiguity, 7–8, 93, 109
Zoom, 125, 131, 140

Books in HIGHER EDUCATION
from HOPKINS PRESS

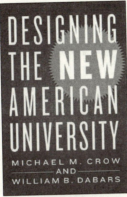

The Fifth Wave
The Evolution of American Higher Education

Michael M. Crow and William B. Dabars

Designing the New American University

Michael M. Crow and William B. Dabars

Academia Next
The Futures of Higher Education

Bryan Alexander

Redesigning Liberal Education
Innovative Design for a Twenty-First-Century Undergraduate Education

edited by William Moner, Phillip Motley, and Rebecca Pope-Ruark
foreword by Michael S. Roth

Alternative Universities
Speculative Design for Innovation in Higher Education

David J. Staley

 JOHNS HOPKINS
UNIVERSITY PRESS

   press.jhu.edu

For more books on HIGHER EDUCATION visit **press.jhu.edu**